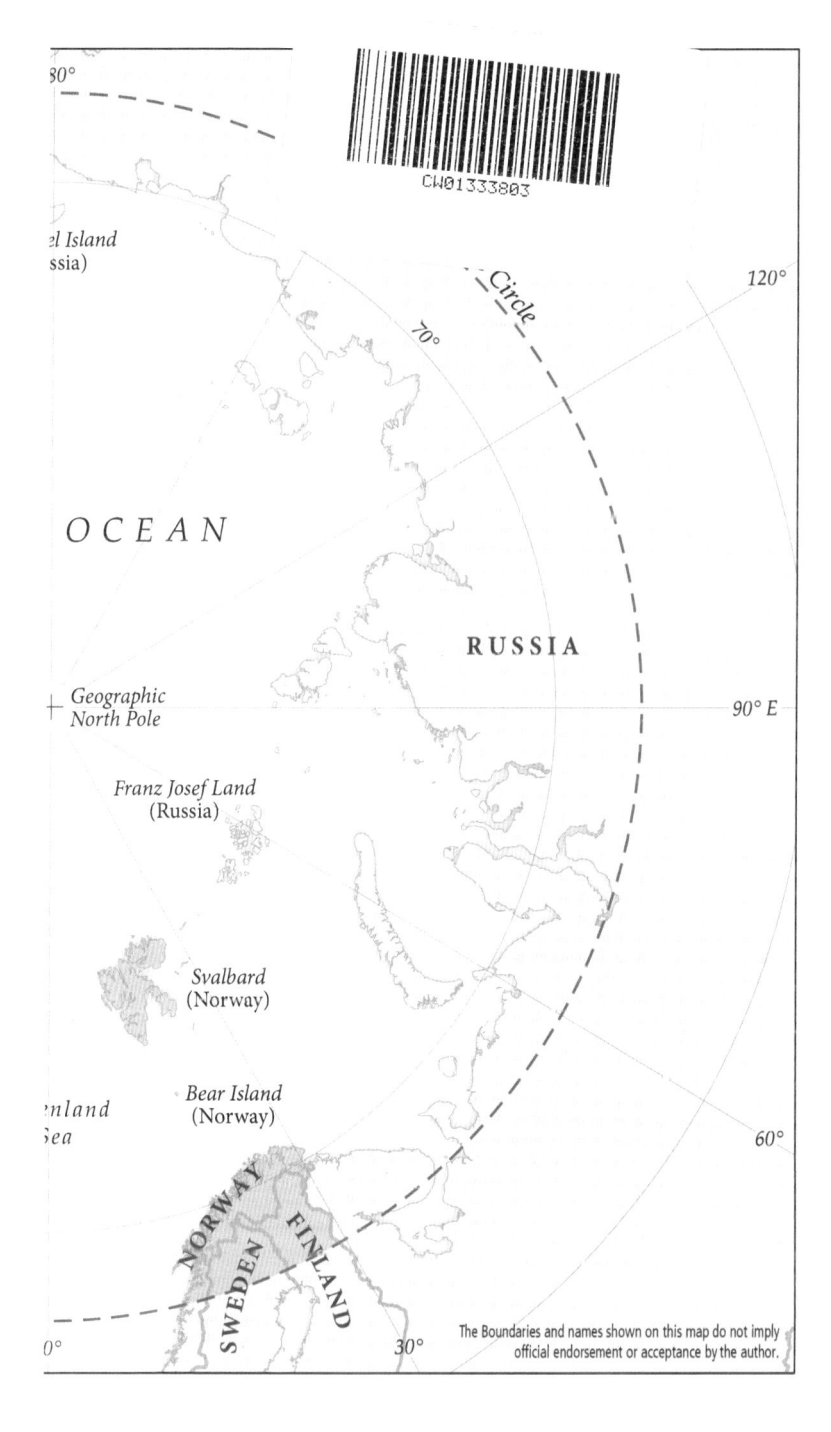

The Boundaries and names shown on this map do not imply official endorsement or acceptance by the author.

'A highly readable (and expert) guide to a remote place that is becoming increasingly important.'
— Gordon Corera, former BBC Security Correspondent, co-host *The Rest is Classified* podcast

'If there is a story of "horrible geopolitics" to be told then Elizabeth Buchanan tells it in her book about Greenland, Grønland and/or Kalaallit Nunaat.'
— Klaus Dodds, Professor of Geopolitics, Royal Holloway, author of, *Inter alia*, *The Arctic: What Everyone Needs to Know*.

'Forget everything you thought you knew about Greenland. Elizabeth Buchanan's *So You Want To Own Greenland?* flips the map on its head, revealing the world's largest island as an unexpected, enduring geopolitical prize. Buchanan unearths Greenland's captivating history in an accessible prose, from the mysterious disappearance of its Viking settlements around the 1400s to Donald Trump's audacious modern-day bid for control. From clandestine Cold War projects like "Iceworm" (a secret underground nuclear city) to the global race for critical minerals, Buchanan dissects the forces shaping Greenland's destiny. She expertly unpacks "lawfare" and "grey-zone activities", revealing China's encroachment and the hidden battles for influence in the High North. This isn't just a history lesson, it's an essential, timely guide to understanding Greenland's complex dance with Denmark, its enduring quest for independence and its pivotal strategic role with the United States in a rapidly changing Arctic. You'll gain a profound appreciation for the island's unique position at the crossroads of North American security and the burgeoning global resource scramble. Insightful, provocative and absolutely indispensable for anyone looking beyond the headlines to grasp the true significance of this crucial Arctic nation. It's the ultimate "buyer's guide" to a land far more vital than most realise.'

— James Kraska, SJD, Charles H Stockton Chair of
International Maritime Law, US Naval War College

'An immensely readable tour through the fascinating history, complicated geopolitics, and long saga of Greenland's relationship with the outside world, especially the United States, including the latest twist with Trump; written by that rare creature, a genuine expert on all things Arctic.'

— Bruce Jones, Director and Senior Fellow in the Project on
International Order and Strategy, the Brookings Institution

'Buchanan offers a cheeky and irreverent guide to the colonial history and possible future of Greenland. But beneath the humorous surface, she delves into important issues of Indigenous rights, domestic politics, maritime and resource concerns, and geostrategic competition. Readers will be both illuminated and entertained.'

— Maria Rost Rublee, Professor of International Relations,
University of Melbourne

'An informative and thought-provoking overview of a timely topic.'

— John McCannon, author of *Red Arctic* and
A History of the Arctic

'From the first Viking colonies, to the intricacies of Danish colonialism, to the first American schemes to take over the island, Buchanan's timely work is a crucial reminder that the future of

Greenland belongs to Greenlanders. It is an essential primer for anyone looking for a breezy yet meticulously researched backgrounder about Greenland.'
— Andrew Chater, Lecturer in Political Science, King's University College, London, Ontario

'One of the least known and understood places on the planet, Greenland sits today at the centre of geopolitical contest for the Arctic. Dr Buchanan does an extraordinary job of providing timely and needed scholarship in a highly entertaining and enjoyable read. I recommend to anyone wishing to know more about this wonderful land and her people.'
— Tom Dans, former US Arctic Research Commissioner

'Elizabeth Buchanan masterfully unpacks Greenland's centuries-long entanglement with empires, opportunists, and would-be buyers. This is a brilliant, bold, witty, and necessary guide to the island's past, present, and uncertain geopolitical future.'
— Patrick J. Sullivan PhD, Director, The Modern War Institute, West Point Military Academy

'Elizabeth Buchanan, with perfect geostrategic timing, has provided us with a very readable and insightful explanation of the history of strategic interest in Greenland and why its location on the map and its expected rich critical mineral deposits make it even more relevant today.'
— Ben Hodges, former Commanding General, United States Army Europe

SO YOU WANT TO OWN GREENLAND?

So You Want to Own Greenland?

Lessons from the Vikings to Trump

ELIZABETH BUCHANAN

HURST & COMPANY, LONDON

First published in the United Kingdom in 2025 by
C. Hurst & Co. (Publishers) Ltd.,
New Wing, Somerset House, Strand, London, WC2R 1LA

© Elizabeth Buchanan, 2025
All rights reserved.

The right of Elizabeth Buchanan to be identified
as the author of this publication is asserted by her in accordance
with the Copyright, Designs and Patents Act, 1988.

A Cataloguing-in-Publication data record for this book
is available from the British Library.

ISBN: 9781805264521

Printed and bound in Great Britain by Bell and Bain Ltd, Glasgow

www.hurstpublishers.com

Contents

Preface		xi
1.	Finding Greenland	1
2.	The Curious Case of the Lost Vikings	7
3.	Dances with Denmark	19
4.	Greenland and the World Wars	41
5.	Project Iceworm	61
6.	Contemporary Geopolitics: Greenlandic Edition	75
7.	All Politics Are Local	93
8.	The Art of a (Green) Deal	123
9.	Four Scenarios	151
Afterword		173
Notes		179
Index		189

Preface

To paraphrase Vladimir Putin: most of us know where Greenland is, but we never think of it. Now, Putin *was* taking a shot at Australia when he muttered these words, but the point is rather apt. Greenland and Australia are both large islands with comparatively small populations dispersed across vast territories. Both are usually at the periphery of day-to-day geopolitics, and neither is regarded as a major power in strategic affairs.

Most of us could locate Greenland on a globe, but few ever think about the island. This was a statement that rang true until the second Trump administration dusted off its Greenland strategy. Dusted off and apparently now on steroids, a refreshed US interest in Greenland has thrust the island to the forefront of global political discourse.

Trump's interest in Greenland is quite straightforward. Indeed, any realist, nay any person armed with a world map, could plainly see the geographic centrality of Greenland to North American security, given that the island is essentially its front doorstep. As with any house, you pay home insurance and invest in a capable security system. This crudely captures the Trump Greenland agenda.

Of course, much of this simple rationale is lost in the noise of an 'America first' era. The Trump administration is not treading lightly, opting instead for brazen soundbites on plans to 'annex' Greenland by force. No doubt, this will continue to undermine policy efforts to strengthen Washington's relationship with Greenland. A colossal own goal for future historians to argue about later.

But it is not all Trump and Co.'s fault. Subject matter expertise on Greenlandic domestic politics is not easily found. Unpacking the nuance of Greenland's local narrative and components of its strategic identity does not lend itself to short news stories or tantalising clickbait tales.

Yet the domestic factors—principally Greenland's quest for independence from Danish rule—are largely pre-existing and pre-Trump processes shaping the political landscape. These developments are generational and not remotely attributable merely to Donald J. Trump.

'Owning' Greenland as a concept is synonymous with the Trump presidency. But it does not originate from Mar-a-Largo. There have been attempts to ignite US interest in securing Greenland since at least 1867. But over 150 years later Washington is still chasing this Greenlandic mirage.

Why is this the case? The US and its formidable war chest cannot capture a military-less nearby island? Despite a legacy of engagement with Greenland, enduring operations there, and clearly signalled intent to invest in a new state-of-the-art home security system, the US has failed to 'own' Greenland.

As this book explores, Washington has from time to time occupied or held Greenland, particularly in times of war. But it has never kept or retained Greenland.

Washington maintains a presence in Greenland, with boots on the ground and a military-intelligence infrastructure at Pituffik Space Base, as well as a diplomatic presence in the nation's capital, Nuuk. Yet, this is still rather short of owning Greenland.

This book illuminates various attempts to 'own' Greenland. From the Viking era to the latest in Trump's designs for Greenland, the book charts the twists and turns of the many quests undertaken to possess the island.

What follows is an examination of several odysseys to retain the island, from Greenland's lost Viking settlement of the 1400s—one of history's great puzzles—to Denmark's struggle to hold onto it. Greenland's gradual transformation from a Danish possession to an autonomous territory is a significant, albeit overlooked, component of the contemporary geopolitical picture.

Few understand the Greenlandic experience with world war, nor its strategic centrality during the Cold War. But these battle scars shaped Greenland and are imprinted on the strategic imagination of North America. Burnt into the psyche of US military-strategic planners is the unparalleled significance of Greenland to homeland security—to the survival of the United States of America. Appreciating this relationship is central to understanding the enduring nature of Washington's interest in Greenland.

Nothing occurs in a vacuum. Greenland now featuring at the forefront of geopolitical debate has coincided with a sharpened focus on the international power balance, fears of China's rise, and growing global resource insecurity.

Mounting domestic pressures in Greenland further compound these external forces. Greenland's independence movement is just one facet here, as socio-economic concerns and environmental threats are further eroding its inhabitants' sense of security.

Through the lens of Trump's intent to 'purchase' Greenland, this book dissects the island's contemporary role and poses four provocative scenarios for its future. Much like Goldilocks, your quest, dear reader, is to decide which scenario seems *just* right.

So, You Want to Own Greenland? As with any home purchase, a buyer must do some serious due diligence. Understand the community, cost any repair work, and suss out your neighbours. Ensure you have a complete conveyancing file at hand—permits, approvals, and prior owners should all be accounted for. Fork out for legal representation, and ensure handsome cash reserves are ready for works needed. In many ways, this book is essentially a buyer's guide to Greenland.

PREFACE

Owning Greenland is an ambitious task. Plenty have tried to possess it, many have occupied it, but few truly understand it. May the odds be ever in your favour.

Elizabeth Buchanan

Canberra, May 2025

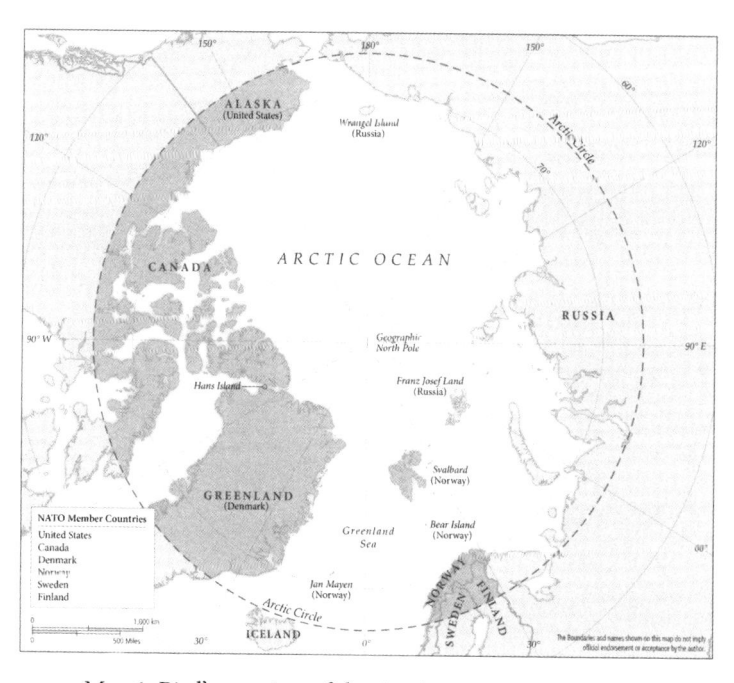

Map 1: Bird's eye view of the Arctic. © Damien Saunder.

1

Finding Greenland

Before venturing to understand the ways in which many have attempted to 'own' Greenland, it is pertinent to be able to find it. As the world's largest island, Greenland is incredibly hard to miss on a world map: big, white, and not at all green. Known as Kalaallit Nunaat (Country of the Greenlanders), the island sits atop the North Atlantic Ocean, reaching into the Arctic Ocean. Most of the island is above the Arctic Circle (see Map 1).

Greenland is about 16 miles (26 kilometres) from Canada—but let's not give Ottawa any ideas. Indeed, the only territorial land dispute above the Arctic Circle for some time was between Canada and Denmark, over Hans Island (marked on Map 1). Between 1973 and 2022 the two nations amicably squabbled over the barren rock (squished between Canada's Ellesmere Island and Greenland). The 'battle' was better known as the 'Whiskey War'—in which each nation routinely traded whiskey bottles atop the centre of the island.[1]

The warring parties struck a deal (back when the United Nations was functioning) in 1973 to settle the overlapping claims. Essentially, the two drew a line down the middle of the barren rock and agreed to arrive at a settlement soon. But it fell far from the top of their national priorities.

For almost fifty years, and quite a few whiskey bottles back and forth (insinuating a claim), come 2022 an agreement was inked. Settlement of the whiskey war saw Hans Island split equally between Canada and Greenland. Denmark led the deliberations and agreement in view of Greenland's semi-autonomous nature, politically speaking.

Discovered in about AD 984 by the exiled Viking Erik the Red, Greenland was home to Europe's most remote outpost until some point in the 1400s. After about 400 years, this entire Norse society vanished from Greenland. But more about this curious case later.

A permanent link between Greenland and the outside world was not established until the Lutheran priest Hans Egede arrived on the island in 1721. Now, our man Hans had intended to convert the Norsemen, but they were long gone. Greenland's Inuit community was instead treated to the teachings of the Lutheran Church. Today, 90 per cent of the Greenlandic population identifies as Inuit, and many are practising Lutherans. Hans's teachings clearly stuck.

Hans's mission to spread the good word also marked what is considered the start of Danish colonisation in Greenland. The island remained a Danish colony until 1953, by 1979 Greenland was granted home rule, and in 2009 it secured self-governing status.

Greenland is a parliamentary democracy. It remains under Danish rule, as part of the Kingdom of Denmark. Greenland's parliament (Inatsisartut) facilitates an autonomous-lite operation, but Denmark retains control over much of foreign and defence affairs. The head of state remains the Danish monarch, while a prime minister represents the Greenlandic people—all 57,000 of them.

Greenland is a self-governing overseas administrative division of Denmark.[2] It is important to understand the complex relationship between these two countries. Any notion of 'owning' Greenland requires a solid grasp of many moving pieces.

Almost two decades ago, the Greenlandic people signalled their *intent* to exit Danish rule for good. A 2008 referendum endorsed a plan that sees Greenland continue to strengthen its autonomy from the Kingdom of Denmark. But this is to be a gradual, glacial process in which Nuuk secures incremental control and responsibility for its affairs. More on this delicate political dance later.

According to the *CIA World Factbook*, the island possesses a rich bounty of natural resources. Coal and hydrocarbons like oil and gas are locked beneath the ice. Critical minerals like lead, zinc, platinum, tantalite and uranium draw global interest to Greenland. The island's living resources—its fisheries—in the waters lapping

Greenland's shores have long held strategic value, as food security internationally continues to erode.[3]

The idea that Greenland is a new entry to the international resource 'race' is misleading. There is a long history of exploration and exploitation of Greenland's mineral riches. Danish firms first held permits beginning in the 1930s, as the world vied for cryolite. Cryolite is a key ingredient in the smelting process to make aluminium. It also makes fireworks yellow. At the time, however, cryolite was coveted for aviation production lines during world war. In 1943, the US naval base Grønnedal opened its doors—right next to Greenland's largest cryolite mine.

Demographically speaking, Greenland is home to a young population, with 40 per cent of people under the age of 30. But population growth is now stagnant. This was not always the case. In the 1960s, Greenland had one of the highest birthrates in the world. Then a policy of forced contraception by the Danish government was rolled out.[4]

Ostensibly, this was a Danish policy to reduce the burgeoning birthrate so as to cut the rising costs carried by Denmark across social and health service provisions. In all, about half of Greenland's fertile women and girls are believed to have received coil implants through to the 1970s at the behest of the Danish government. In 2022, the governments of Denmark and Greenland launched a formal investigation into the programme, on the back of some 140 Greenlandic women coming forward to sue the Danish government. Greenland's domestic political scene has been far from quiet.

Greenland's physical environment is also on the move. Eighty per cent of the Greenland landmass is covered in ice—ice that is melting. According to NASA, between 2002 and 2023 Greenland lost about 270 billion metric tons of ice per year.[5] Most of the ice loss has been in West Greenland, the most populous part of the island. Of course, the impact of climate change can often be a matter of perspective.

The melting Greenlandic icesheet has disrupted communities—hunting grounds are difficult to reach, fisheries are moving, and permafrost threatens the longevity of existing infrastructure across the island. But the melting icecap has also made the prospecting, extraction, and exploitation of critical minerals easier. This attracts vast interest in the economic potential of Greenland. More on the geostrategic lure of Greenland and her mineral wealth later.

A final note on finding Greenland—for the flat-earthers among us. True, Greenland is the world's largest island. However, maps distort its true size. Simply blame a guy from the 1500s—Mr Mercator. Greenland is *not* the size of Africa. It is roughly three times the size of France, or one West Australia.

Now, for the curious case of the missing Greenlandic Vikings.

2

The Curious Case of the Lost Vikings

Our first tale of an attempt to 'own' Greenland concerns the Vikings. In around AD 982, an enterprising (albeit murderous) man—Erik the Red—conjured the name Greenland. He did so to lure fellow Vikings to settle on Greenland, with its connotations of lush, rich soil, prime and ready for prosperous settlements to flourish. Indeed, salesmen are the same, no matter the century.

Now, picture Ed Sheeran's head, with a lush siren-red full beard, atop André the Giant's body. Meet Erik the Red. What we know of Erik the Red is like much of the Viking fables, or sagas, written hundreds of years after the fact. So, details are often sketchy. Vikings were known for their pillaging, warring, and general raiding or plundering social activities.

Erik the Red was no different. Born Erik Thorvaldsson around AD 950 in Norway, he joined his banished father and grew up in Iceland. His father had caused the family to be exiled from Norway as punishment for manslaughter. Like father, like son, it would seem. A grown Erik killed his neighbour and was slapped with a three-year exile sentence for manslaughter. Erik took to the sea and opted to explore the lands west of Iceland to kill the time. It was during this period he discovered Greenland. After years of charting and exploration, Erik returned to Iceland to sell the allure of Greenland. Famine had hit Iceland at the time, so it was not necessarily a difficult proposition for many.

About 25 boats, with up to 500 people, followed Erik and set sail for Greenland. The treacherous sea conditions meant roughly 10 boats were lost on the journey. The Vikings set about establishing two colonies in about AD 985 in the south of Greenland. The Western Settlement was the smaller of the two, located around the fjords of modern-day Nuuk. The Eastern Settlement spanned much of southern Greenland and was home to considerably more Vikings. At their height, the Viking colonies in Greenland swelled to about 2,500 people.

Viking life in Greenland was not just a tale of isolation on an icesheet. Farms sprang up across the settlements they now called home, and here the Vikings worked the arable land. Livestock introduced to Greenland by the Vikings included cattle, sheep, and goats.

Trade, specifically the movement of goods across seas, is key for global prosperity and security. This is a long-standing basic tenet of the world, and something the Vikings also had to deal with. The Greenland Viking colonies amassed their wealth primarily through trade in ivory from walrus tusks and furs from seals.

Those savvy Norwegian kings cottoned on to the riches of Greenland. As did the Church. Between the two, Europe's ivory trade was monopolised by Norway (by way of the Greenlandic Vikings). According to most historical accounts, things remained peachy for our Viking friends for quite some time.

Not so much for Erik. Erik the Red died in about AD 1003, from something unbefitting a man of his stature or reputation—he simply fell off a horse. Or caught a virus from new Viking settlers. Both stories feature in the history books.

Greenland's Viking colonies prospered for some 500 years. And then they were gone. According to the Smithsonian Institution, three letters were written by Viking colonists between 1409 and 1424. Luckily they were subsequently archived by prudent scribes.[1] These letters are the last official word from Greenland's Vikings. They tell of a marriage and a witch burning. Utterly devoid of scandal, these were apparently two different events—the bride was not tried for witchcraft.

But it is what is *not* in the letters that is even more perplexing. There are no mentions of brewing societal unrest or financial or security troubles in the colony. The Vikings of Greenland went quiet, and apparently no

Europeans ventured to visit, either. If they did, it was to no Viking welcome. The two settlements were ghost towns.

Remember our man Hans Egede? The Protestant priest set sail from Norway in 1721 to check in with the Vikings on Greenland. After all, it had been a few hundred years since anyone had heard from the colonies in Greenland. No news of weddings (or witch burnings) was certainly not good news. Hans arrived instead to crumbling farms and Inuit shrugs, which indicated 'those guys left years ago'.

Just like Carrie Bradshaw, Hans couldn't help but wonder … *what happened to the Vikings?* His journal account asked: 'What has been the fate of so many human beings, so long cut off from all intercourse with the more civilized world?'[2] Grim reading. Accounting for the missing Viking colonies has become, quite literally, a professional occupation. Anthropologists and historians have spent decades scouring Greenland for answers. They continue to do so.

Answers to the curious case of the missing Vikings range from starvation to conflict, to arguments that they just 'up and left'. Scant stories of alien involvement appear from time to time. There are many possible answers to the mystery, although none have been categorically agreed to by the experts. Hot off the heels of our global Covid-19 pandemic, let's first consider the plague. Did new colonists bring the Black Death to Greenland's Viking community?

Indeed, the Black Death was busy devastating the world in the fourteenth century. By 1356 it had killed a quarter of

Europe's population.[3] Trade with Norway at the time was crucial for Viking colony survival. Knowing about 60 per cent of Norway's population was lost to the bubonic plague, it is reasonable to argue that the Black Death did reach Greenland's shores and work its way through the Viking colonies. However, the absence (to date) of mass graves, or any archaeological evidence of plague reaching the community, indicates the Black Death probably did not wipe out the Vikings.

After plague, war. Or so the saying goes. War is, of course, another popular narrative accounting for the missing Greenlandic Vikings. Did they perish in a heated battle with the Inuit? There are certainly some echoes here of England's lost settlement at Roanoke in North America. Did the Viking colony fail to make nice with the Inuit? The historical record recounts various run-ins with the local Greenlandic Inuit during the early Viking days. But these stories recall spars mostly around seal and walrus hunting grounds on culturally significant fjord zones. Archaeologists have yet to find evidence of any large, colony-ending battle near or in the central Viking settlement areas.

Maybe we should follow the money? Economic collapse could have forced the Vikings to pack it in and head back to Norway. By about 1261, the Vikings of Greenland had made a deal to come under the Norwegian Crown in return for dedicated trade relations. Researchers note the last ivory trade ship to sail from Greenland left in about 1369.[4]

Around this time African ivory was unlocked, so, thanks to globalisation, isolated Greenlandic walrus ivory was no longer economically competitive. Once elephant ivory made its way into the market, the Greenlandic Vikings' primary export (and currency) was annihilated. Not only was a competitor product flooding the market, but various trade routes that were then opening ensured the long-term diversification of the ivory trade.

However, the history books lack reference to any 'major' influx of Vikings returning home. Surely stories of boatloads of defeated Vikings returning home from Greenland would have made the news—or reached the dedicated scribes of the time.

Indeed, Greenland's Viking settlements could simply have left the island. A mass exodus to North America, or back to their Nordic heartland, is possible. But this is unlikely. The areas around the Eastern and Western Settlements weren't (and aren't) home to large trees. We know this because Vikings built their communities—homes, churches, farms, meeting halls—out of stone, not wood.

This is an important point, given that when Europeans ventured to check in on the long-silent Vikings, they did not find the settlements in disarray. There was no evidence of conflict, nor any semblance of a rushed exit out of town. Churches and homes had been stripped of personal effects and trimmings.

Say the Vikings took their belongings, accumulated over centuries, with them, how on earth did they transport everything? The few boats left for the colonists required imported wood and parts—fabric for sails—to keep afloat. But we know that Greenlandic trade had ceased for quite some time. With no trees to build any new boats to leave the island, where did the masses of personal effects get to? And how would the many hundreds of Vikings get off the island?

The most popular answer to the question of the missing Vikings tends to be climate change. Did a changing climate make life too hard for the settlers to work the land, and grow and sustain crops or livestock? Today, scientists with advanced technologies have uncovered some interesting data to support the climate thesis.

One study, aptly titled 'Prolonged drying trend coincident with the demise of Norse settlement in southern Greenland', found the climate wasn't too cold, or that a 'new' ice age hadn't consumed Greenland.[5] Researchers instead discovered that a drought hit Greenland during its Viking era.

The scientists drilled into the grounds of the Eastern Settlement and found the late fourteenth century was one of the warmest periods in Greenland's entire climate record. Researchers concluded there was no 'abrupt' drop in temperature for Greenland at the time. Rather, each summer of the Vikings' residency in Greenland became more and more dry.

This evidence counters other climate arguments related to the demise of the Vikings of Greenland. Some experts believe sea levels rose around Greenland, causing vast flooding of Viking settlements. The conclusion is that the rising sea levels and ensuing floods destroyed the existing Viking communities.

Researchers also uncovered human remains in Viking burial grounds which point to a clear shift away from livestock to marine-life diets for the settlers.[6] This major dietary change supports the notion that access to arable land to raise livestock forced the Vikings to follow the footsteps of the Inuit and look to the sea for sustenance.

All we know for sure is that by the fifteenth century over 2,000 humans had vanished. In our quest for answers a blend of all the suspected reasons for the missing Greenlandic Vikings sounds about right. Illness and death may have wiped them out. The concentrated nature of the two Viking settlements made for easy communication and, of course, easy circulation of communicable illnesses.

Conflict with the Inuit is also likely. A cursory review of the 'Norse annals' uncovers three cases of Viking–Inuit clashes in Greenland, all of which resulted in absolute bloodshed.[7] But no tales have been handed down in the history books of a colony-ending war.

The collapse of Viking society in Greenland could very well have been spurred by economic disaster. We know dire economic times hit the Greenlandic Vikings when their primary export—ivory—became rather worthless. New precious materials took its place—gold and diamonds. (Much later came US treasury bonds.) For the Vikings on Greenland there was relatively little to pivot to for export. After all, there are only so many seal pelts Vikings can hawk.

There is merit in examining the notion that the Vikings just split Greenland in the middle of night. Until we consider the logistics of such an operation. Or the fact that our buddy Hans Egede reported shock and awe when arriving at a Viking-less settlement or two. Surely if the Greenlandic Vikings had 'left' the island and returned home, there'd be no need to send a reconnaissance mission to 're-establish' communications?

Environmental factors probably did facilitate, in one way or another, the demise of the Greenlandic Vikings. Whether through drought or flood, or a new ice age, the precarious nature of Greenland's climate would have been an enduring determinant of the settlements' day-to-day life—and prosperity, as well as their long-term viability. Over many centuries how did the Vikings fail to adapt? Surely the communities learnt to follow the Inuit example.

The Vikings were known best for their raiding, plundering, and pillaging extracurricular activities. But they were also clever, enterprising, brave people. Renowned for their seafaring, questing, and conquering of nature, and the discovery of new lands, the Vikings made their mark on the world. Netflix smash-hit shows, as well as Norse mythology and legend, ensure the Vikings remain infused in popular culture today. This makes the curious case of the missing Viking colony in Greenland even more tantalising.

The Vikings were skilled shipbuilders, navigators, and tamers of the wild sea. They were known to explore and colonise. Modern society is even built upon the blueprint of a Viking settlement, in which trade and economy are crucial to the functioning of a community led by a top-down order. Despite all these strengths, and evidence of enduring societies elsewhere at the time, it is rightly concerning that no explicit explanation exists in the annals of history to account for the demise of Erik's colonies.

To make an educated guess, the Vikings of Greenland very likely simply died out. A slow end, with the dwindling settlements under siege from within. To paraphrase Hemingway, Greenland's Viking community most likely collapsed in two ways: gradually, then suddenly. Incidentally, the Hemingway family name also has Viking roots, with Norse settlers in Scotland.[8] But I digress.

So, you want to own Greenland? There are evident lessons from the Vikings' attempt to do so. First and foremost, have a plan B (and C to Z). Diversify your options to ensure a sustained and prosperous lifestyle on the island. Bring your own food. Invest in your defences. Bolster your alliances and partnerships beyond the island. Accept you are not the first custodians of the island. Acknowledge historical attempts to settle on Greenland have not been straightforward or without difficulty.

This means potential buyers, our new-age Viking colonisers, must do some serious due diligence before making the move. What are they getting into with Greenland? Know the land, know the people, and know the history. Even back in the actual Viking era, Inuit knew the land, they were nomadic and moved throughout the island as the seasons changed. They adapted and worked in partnership with the land. Where Vikings had a meat-heavy diet, relied on livestock, and operated from a fixed-settlement location, the Inuit had a seafood-heavy diet and rotated between fishery grounds, careful not to overfish.

The Vikings of Greenland do deserve more pages in our history books. It might have been a fleeting colony, but it had significant implications for the world as we know it today. In this vein, let's close the chapter with a short reflection on *legacy*. The actions, policies, grand plans, or vibes that one may have today for Greenland will no doubt have long-term implications in future history books.

After all, if Erik the Red didn't relocate to Greenland, establish a colony, and raise his family, then America might not have been discovered. Erik's son Leif Erikson is said to have sailed to North America in AD 1000—long before old mate Christopher Columbus. In 1964, US President Lyndon Johnson went so far as to proclaim 9 October 'Leif Erikson Day' to commemorate the discovery.[9]

The most perplexing aspect of the curious case of the missing Greenlandic Vikings is the absence of their legacy in contemporary US strategic discussions. Greenland and the US are strange bedfellows, but bedfellows nonetheless. Let's now consider what happens with three in the bed, by exploring the Denmark–Greenland relationship.

3

Dances with Denmark

The most successful story (to date) of 'owning' Greenland is that of the Danes. In terms of relationship status, the Denmark–Greenland one remains 'complicated'. Neither likes putting a label on it. Greenland often threatens to leave, and Denmark reminds her who pays the bills. Denmark is fully committed, they have some serious history, while Greenland is in her 'independent woman' era. Officially, and on public profiles, Greenland is an autonomous, self-governing yet dependent territory of the Danish realm.

Trigger warning: this chapter delves into the dirty 'c' word. No, not that one. *Colonialism*. But, first, some history. What follows is a short history of the Greenland–Denmark relationship, one that is by no means exhaustive. The twists and turns of history—from nineteenth-century European power shifts, to revolutions, the influence of that (little) guy Napoleon, and bubbling twentieth-century tensions—are all covered at length elsewhere.[1]

As discussed in the previous chapter, Viking settlements spanned the southern end of Greenland from about 986 to 1450, give or take a few years. Greenland's Inuit population came across from North America in about 1200 and remained rather nomadic for centuries. Historians believe up to six different Inuit cultures made their way to Greenland, with the current Inuit population being descendants of the last migration wave—the Thule culture.[2]

International intrigue over Greenland has waxed and waned for centuries. For a hot minute in the fifteenth century, Portugal laid claim to Greenland. This claim was based on the Treaty of Tordesillas—the 1494 agreement between the Spanish and Portuguese to carve the world into two spheres of influence.[3] Greenland simply fell within the Portuguese sphere. But the claim was never acted upon.

Then in 1721, our Danish-Norwegian missionary man, Hans Egede, lobbied the King of Demark–Norway (Frederick IV) for permission to venture out to Greenland.[4] The colonisation of Greenland began with his arrival, and the ripples remain today. As examined in the previous chapter, Hans received no Viking welcome. Instead, he set about sharing the Lutheran 'Word' with the Inuit. And share the Word he did—today over 90 per cent of Greenlanders belong to the Lutheran Church.[5]

Greenland was next rocked by external political forces during the Napoleonic Wars of the early 1800s. Napoleon had spent considerable energy masterminding the rise of

France, causing a domino effect of shifting alliances throughout Europe. Specifically relevant to Greenland was the 1814 Treaty of Kiel.

This treaty ended hostilities that had erupted between Sweden and Denmark during this period thanks to Napoleon.[6] In doing so, Denmark handed Norway to Sweden. Denmark, however, kept Greenland, Iceland, and the Faroe Islands. Norway's Viking-era links to Greenland and the ties cultivated by missionary Hans Egede were abruptly cut by the Danes.

In 1867, Washington came knocking. The United States (US) apparently approached Denmark with an interest in purchasing Greenland. US Secretary of State William Seward was hot off the heels of his most recent territorial purchase—Alaska from Russia. Dubbed a 'folly' at the time, specifically the 'Seward folly', further negotiations to secure Greenland simply lost momentum.

In 1905 Norway gained independence from Sweden. This kicked off another chapter in Greenland's geopolitical history. Norway never recognised the Treaty of Kiel, which had handed Greenland to Denmark, and held firmly to its own historical claim to the island.

Washington's interest in Greenland was piqued again in 1910. This time, the US Ambassador to Denmark saw the opportunity. Ambassador Egan shared his shrewd plan to get Greenland into the hands of the US; it just required a convoluted 'three-way' trade deal. The plan went something like this: step one, Denmark cedes Greenland to the US; next, Washington hands Denmark a few islands in the Philippines; then, Denmark offers said islands to Germany, which would result in Germany handing back the territory of Schleswig-Holstein which it had won in war from Denmark.[7] One too many moving parts for the Americans, it would seem, and the plan fizzled.

Of course, islands did change hands elsewhere. The Danes may have previously rebuffed Washington's bid to buy Greenland, but in 1917 it sold what was known as the Danish West Indies (the Virgin Islands) to the US.[8] These islands had been under Danish control since the late 1600s, but Washington eyed their proximity to the Panama Canal. Ultimately, the US paid $25 million (in gold coins) for the Danish West Indies. Some mighty fine precedent.

In 1921 Denmark turned up the heat in the debate over who 'owns' Greenland. The Danish parliament strengthened its control over the island by declaring foreigners needed permission to set foot on Greenland. Norway, still not a fan of the Treaty of Kiel, did not take kindly to this development.

Then, a decade later, in 1931, Norway simply annexed an eastern slice of Greenland. The coastal area from Carlsberg Fjord to Bessel Fjord, to be exact. The thinking in Oslo was essentially that Norway had long-held historical ties to the island (remember our friend Erik the Red and fellow Norse Vikings?) and should have a say in Greenland's future. If not that, a share of the riches. Furthermore,

Norway argued that Denmark only had claim to the populated zones in the south of the island. Apparently, the Norwegians planned to deploy their (dilapidated) navy to back up their own claim.

In July 1932, Norway issued a royal decree proclaiming the slice of annexed Greenland to be 'Eirik Raudes Land' (Erik the Red's Land).[9] Henceforth this would be known as Norwegian territory. Both parties talked the big talk, but no shots were fired. Instead, rational thinking prevailed—with Denmark and Norway turning to the Permanent Court of International Justice (PCIJ) in The Hague to resolve their spat over eastern Greenland.

Both parties ventured to The Hague for arbitration in 1933. The PCIJ ruled in favour of Denmark and her established sovereignty over the entire island of Greenland.[10] Norway simply abandoned its claim upon acceptance of the court's ruling. Both even split the costs of the proceedings. All rather adult of them really.

Greenland's next brush with external geopolitical forces came in the form of the Nazis. With the fall of Denmark in 1940, Greenland was again adrift. But more on this era in the next chapter.

In 1953 Greenland broke free from its colonial chains. She became a district of the Danish realm. But politics still reared their ugly head. An enduring discourse of independence and the promise of future autonomy for the Greenlandic people were written into the 1979 Home Rule

Act. As a result Greenland picked up some serious political power.

As Peter Parker, best known as Spider-Man, says, 'with great power comes great responsibility'. And this was certainly true for Greenland. While the Greenlandic people secured a louder voice in their own affairs, it was not without cost and growing challenge.

According to the Library of Congress, the Home Rule Act entered into force thanks to a referendum in Greenland which saw 70.1 per cent of voters (based on a 63 per cent voter turnout) support 'increased autonomy' from Denmark.[11]

According to the Home Rule Act, Greenland assumed responsibility for eight policy areas, including areas like local governance, the Church, teaching and cultural affairs. Areas such as the judiciary and courts, police and prison services remained a Danish responsibility.

The Home Rule Act was essentially a quest for greater political and economic independence for Greenland.[12] The Act established Greenland as 'a distinct community within the Kingdom of Denmark'. It enabled Greenland to acquire its own governance assembly (called the Landsting), to be administered by an executive (the Landsstyre). Members of the Landsstyre would be elected for four-year terms.

The assembly (Landsting) was afforded latitude to make its own standing orders and was handed the authority to enact and implement the Home Rule Act in Greenland.

When it comes to the powers that fall under the Act, things get interesting. In many ways, the items that came under the Home Rule schedule read like a shopping list for 'Democracy 101', perhaps even a 'Dummies' Guide to Running a Nation'. The Act made provisions for Greenlanders to organise local government, apply and collect taxes, establish churches and deal with new religious communities, oversee fishing, hunting, agriculture, conservation and environmental protection efforts, and undertake country planning.

Greenlanders could also fill their boots with legislation. The Home Rule Act turned the island into a nirvana for legislators. The Act enabled Greenland to create its own legislation for trade and competition, from hospitality to tourism (and everything in between) and even shop hours. In addition, it could pass laws for social welfare, health services, the labour market, education and cultural affairs, economic development and the supply of goods to the island, as well as the internal transport network.

Quite a list of responsibilities was transferred to Greenland. Save for the striking absence of anything related to foreign policy, military security, or defence affairs. Those tasks appeared to remain well within the remit of Danish power. Section 11 of the Act set out succinctly the envisioned way this would work. Foreign affairs would remain squarely Denmark's business. Policy intent or measures under consideration by Greenlandic authorities under the Home Rule Act, should they have 'substantial importance for the foreign relations of the Realm', required discussion with Denmark first.

Whether or not something is 'substantial' is largely a matter of perspective. Greenland offering to partner with Canada to build and operate a critical mineral mine is probably of less *substantial* political concern than if, say, China is the partner. Likewise, a bilateral fishing partnership with Norway is of probably less *substantial* importance for Danish foreign affairs. Whereas a Greenland–Russia fishing venture might result in robust discussions with Denmark prior to signing a deal. Obviously, the Trump matter falls under 'substantial importance'—more on this later.

In the fine print of the Home Rule Act, Section 4(2) to be exact, Greenlandic authorities not only received power over the items listed above but, once they were transferred, so was the cost. All transfer of authority involved full responsibility 'for expenditure associated' to be taken by Greenland.

How exactly was Greenland to foot the bill? Sitting atop vast resource wealth, critical minerals, and hydrocarbons, as well as national waters rich in fisheries, Greenland certainly had the capacity to fill its coffers. It just lacked the capability to do so. This is still very much Greenland's problem today.

The question of who 'owns' Greenland's alluring resource base was also dealt with by the Home Rule Act. Section 8 of the Act stated that 'the resident population of Greenland has fundamental rights in respect of Greenland's natural resources'. Things are a little grey thereafter.

To protect the 'interests of the unity of the Realm', where 'Realm' is Danish for Denmark, the Faroe Islands, and Greenland, the Act set out that 'preliminary study, prospecting and the exploitation of these resources are to be regulated by agreement' between Denmark and Greenland. Freedom to control the wealth beneath Greenlandic feet, but only to a point, it would seem.

Culturally, for Greenlandic peoples the Act was monumental. Greenlandic was recognised by the Home Rule Act as the principal language of the nation, although Danish was to be 'thoroughly taught'.

Beyond an utter absence of Greenlandic agency in foreign affairs or defence and security, the Home Rule Act also had a few binding requirements that further kneecapped the notion of absolute autonomy. Greenland was to be bound by the same obligations stemming from treaties or international agreements entered into by Denmark. The Act ensured the Danes could direct Greenlandic authorities to observe all obligations to international authorities as necessary.

Some aspects of the Home Rule Act did try to ensure autonomy. Autonomy is about having the freedom to govern or control your own affairs. Greenland gets this, to a point, but not entirely given the good number of pesky caveats. While Greenland is handed control over many aspects of day-to-day life, Section 12 of the Act highlights various avenues through which Denmark still possesses the power to hand down administrative statutes or orders. Any bills or orders emanating from Denmark are simply referred to Greenlandic authorities for their 'comments before they are introduced'. Even new treaties signed by Denmark, where they impact on Greenland, are merely referred for comment by the Greenlandic people 'before being put into force'.

Of course, autonomy is not the same as independence. Independence is about freedom from outside control, not being subject to another's authority, not depending on another for livelihood, capable of thinking for oneself, existing separate from another. None of this was happening for Greenland.

It would seem neither autonomy nor independence was possible through the Home Rule Act. Luckily for Greenland, another Act was about to debut. After Greenland had endured a quarter of a century of home rule, its desire for self-governance was recognised by Denmark. In 2004 the Greenland premier and the Danish prime minister came together to sign the terms of reference for Greenland's march towards bolstered autonomy.

The Greenlandic–Danish Self-Government Commission was established to craft the new Act.[13] The commission's report was delivered and made publicly available in April 2008. The terms of reference are worth examining. The report set down that 'the Commission shall, on the basis of

Greenland's present constitutional position and in accordance with the right of self-determination of the people of Greenland under international law, deliberate and make proposals for how the Greenland authorities can assume further powers, where this is constitutionally possible'.

Now for the cynical part. It continues: 'independence will have to be implemented through the conclusion of an agreement … under the rules laid down in section 19 of the Danish Constitution'. Evidently, any proposal suggested by the commission towards securing Greenland's independence would have to satisfy the Danish Constitution.

Time for a quick refresher on the Danish Constitution. Well, maybe just Section 19. This stipulates that (1) 'The King shall act on behalf of the Realm in international affairs. Provided that without the consent of the Parliament the King shall not undertake any act whereby the territory of the Realm will be increased or decrease'; (2) 'Except for purposes of defence against an armed attack upon the Realm or Danish forces the King shall not use military force against any foreign state without the consent of the Parliament'; and (3) 'The Parliament shall appoint from among its Members a Foreign Affairs Committee, which the Government shall consult prior to the making of any decision of major importance to foreign policy'.

So, any pathway for Greenland's independence tabled by the Foreign Affairs Committee must be able to clear the

Danish parliament for consent to decrease the size of the realm. Should Greenland seek external support to break away—say, a friendly supporter in Washington—the Danes could not use military force to defend Greenland unless parliament came together and consented to do so. Finally, lovers of committees rejoice, the Danish Foreign Affairs Committee must be consulted prior to any decision being taken on Greenland 'exiting' the realm.

Curly processes aside, Greenland's Act on Self-Government was put to a referendum. Held on 25 November 2008, the referendum approved the Greenland Self-Government Act. Some thirty years on from the Home Rule Act referendum, support for increased autonomy remained high in the island. In fact, support had grown. The 2008 referendum (with a voter turnout of almost 72 per cent) saw 75 per cent of Greenlanders seeking increased independence.[14]

The 2008 referendum itself was quite straightforward. Voters were asked to answer yes or no to the question 'Do you want self-government to be introduced in Greenland with the content and conditions outlined in the Greenland–Danish Self-Government Commission's draft self-government Act?'

In 2009, the Act on Greenland Self-Government (AGSG) replaced the Home Rule Act.[15] By this means, the autonomy versus independence conundrum was (arguably) resolved by AGSG. In essence, it was a more robust attempt to expand autonomy and clear the way for the Greenlandic people's right to decide the terms of their independence.

Self-determination was at the heart of AGSG. It underscored an agreement between the Danish government and Greenland's home authority that the possibility of independence for the island (and the way in which such a course would be charted) was a right that sat squarely with the Greenlandic people. Significantly, the Act recognised Greenland as a *distinct nation* under international law.

In practice, AGSG expanded many of the responsibilities already transferred under the 1979 Home Rule Act. More control was handed over across a suite of domestic affairs. Of course, one key development was increased Greenlandic control over natural resources and strategic minerals.

Through AGSG, the nation assumed essentially three more 'core' competencies for self-management. These included the control or administration of justice and courts of law in Greenland, the police, and broadened rights over mineral and oil resources. The exact transfer schedule included industrial injury compensation, remaining healthcare responsibilities, policing of roads and traffic areas, property law, and the establishment of commercial diving zones.

Under AGSG further transfers of duties from Danish administration to Greenland included prison and probation services, passport creation, criminal law, border control, family and succession law, maritime emergency services, aviation, intellectual property, copyright, ship registration, charting, marine environments, financial regulation, and meteorology services.

Economic relations between Greenland and Denmark were also beefed up by AGSG. An annual subsidy of 3.4 billion Danish crowns (about US$325 million) was granted. While based on 2009 price and wage levels, this subsidy is adjusted annually. The Greenlandic language was announced as the official language, sans any reference to the need to promote the Danish language (as the Home Rule Act did).

There were obvious exemptions—affairs remaining under the remit of the Danish government. Foreign affairs, defence and security policy, the constitution, the Supreme Court, concerns of nationality, exchange rates, and broader monetary policy were all items that stayed under Danish control.

Some transfer of responsibilities in the foreign affairs sphere was granted by AGSG, though they were quite meagre. For example, Greenland can act in international affairs, but not in any way that might limit Denmark's 'responsibility and powers'. Greenland can also negotiate (on behalf of the Danish realm) on affairs that 'exclusively concern Greenland *and* entirely relate to fields of responsibility taken over'. Arctic marine environmental concerns would fit this bill, but negotiating an alliance with Iran would probably not.

Reiterated at length in the 2009 Act is the idea that all decisions on Greenlandic independence are to be taken by the people of Greenland. The Danish and Greenlandic parliaments accept this unequivocally. *How* Greenland secures independence, however, is a much murkier affair. This is an obvious tension.

When it comes to securing Greenlandic independence, the 2009 Act, Section 21, outlines everything, and nothing, all at once. And it goes like this. Any decision to seek independence is simply one to be taken by the people of Greenland. If they take such a decision, then negotiations between Denmark and Greenland kick off 'with a view to the introduction of independence'— whatever that means. Next, an agreement from these negotiations must be struck and this agreement is to be endorsed by a referendum in Greenland. Seems straightforward enough, right? The Act continues by stating that any agreement shall be 'concluded with the consent of the Folketing' (Danish parliament).

Even for those fluent in legal mumbo jumbo, the idea that an agreement struck and bolstered by a referendum *still* requires 'consent' from Denmark feels anything but independent. Further, the Act's section on Greenland's purported access to independence states: 'Independence for Greenland shall imply that Greenland assumes sovereignty over the Greenland territory.' Again, to 'imply' sovereignty seems rather loose terminology. Law is often about interpretation, and any shrewd individual can see the wriggle room built into the 2009 Act.

The 2009 Act simply meant that Greenland moved from home rule to self-rule. A change in name, sure, but in practice? More like autonomy with stringent qualifications. Greenland's pathway to independence, lit by AGSG, is not something promised. And while a process was agreed to, the Act does not necessarily frame Greenlandic independence as inevitable.

Perhaps the point of AGSG was rather for Denmark and Greenland to take the opportunity to reinforce their intertwined relationship. After all, the Act included a dedication by both to cultivate equality and mutual respect between the two nations.

Independence has been much like a carrot dangled by Denmark. While a pathway to independence was acknowledged in the latest parliamentary Act, one can't help wondering if the goalposts continue to shift just out of reach.

From the Danish perspective, Greenland is a critical component of the Danish realm. No longer a colony, not really a district, Greenland is treated as an autonomous Danish territory. At least that is what's on the label. Digging deeper and reviewing the political instruments (or Acts) used to facilitate the Danish–Greenlandic relationship, it appears the notion of 'autonomy' is flimsy at best.

The Greenlandic position is complicated. The small size of the population (about 57,000 people) limits the economic potential and power of the national workforce. Without economic power, it is difficult to secure self-sufficiency, and this is certainly a precondition for establishing independence from Denmark. For this reason, the AGSG is probably the best that the Greenlandic people could hope for. A clear space for self-government has been carved out by Greenland, with the long-term quest for independence not off the table either. But even stepping along the pathway to independence, through gaining greater autonomy, Greenland needs to resource the burden.

Denmark coyly remains a fervent supporter of Greenlandic autonomy and self-government. Indeed, the Danes are quick to use AGSG to point to their support for Greenland's independence. But they certainly don't make it easy. With the pathway bogged down in process and legal loopholes which involve the Danish Constitution, Denmark doesn't plan to make Greenland's pursuit of independence an easy one. After all, the Danes *could* just let Greenland leave the realm. But something tells me that card is not on the table.

Nonetheless, the mirage of progress and partnership between Denmark and Greenland endures. Now, this lot certainly like commissions. Indeed, between the two, many a commission has bloomed. There is the 2000 Self-Government Commission, the 2004 Danish Greenlandic

Self-Government Commission, a 2014 Reconciliation Committee (although the Danes refused to join this one), the 2017 Constitutional Commission, and, of course, the 2022 Commission into the Historical Ties Between Denmark and Greenland.[16]

The work of the 2017 Constitutional Commission is most intriguing. Not least because the resulting draft of the Greenlandic constitution for an independent, sovereign state was not even made public until 2023.

Greenland's draft constitution serves to lay the foundation for a sovereign state.[17] It essentially builds upon the 2009 AGSG, which affords the Greenlandic people the right to attain independence—via a referendum and, then, Danish approval. The draft constitution emphasises the maintenance of a democratic system of governance for Greenland with human rights and environmental protection at the centre. A hallmark of the document is recognition of Inuit heritage and the Greenlandic language.

The draft constitution skirts over the more functional aspects of sovereignty—those pesky laws and administrative duties. Will Greenland have its own judicial system, separate citizenship processes, and passport once independent? These are unresolved in the draft constitution. Also missing from the document is the role of the Danish monarchy. Does Greenland seek to become a republic? In the annex of the draft constitution there appears to be discussion of a free association agreement between Denmark and Greenland.

This would take care of Greenland's vast defence and security needs.

Of course, the purpose of the exercise undertaken by the Constitutional Commission was simply to spark national debate. It was a necessary addition to the Greenlandic discourse on independence and served to expose evident gaps between the want and will of Greenland and the practical (economic capacity) limits it operates within.

The independence dream remains alive and well for Greenland. A January 2025 poll found that 56 per cent of Greenlanders would vote yes in a referendum to leave Denmark, 28 per cent would vote no, and 17 per cent do not know whether they'd vote yes or no.[18] Of interest in this survey is the fact that a small majority of voters agree that Denmark should, even once Greenland is independent, continue to support it financially. Awkward.

At once Greenland has its own language, cultural identity, and flag. Greenland's flag is evidence of a concerted effort to depart from its Danish ties and celebrate its independence. It is said that parliament (Inatsisartut) voted for the red-and-white flag over a proposed green-and-white cross design. The rest of the realm has cross-centric flags; indeed, all Scandinavian countries (Finland, Iceland, Norway, and Sweden) feature the offset cross. But beyond the flag, independence is fleeting for Greenland.

Denmark continues to foot the bill for Greenland's public health system, its education department, and the national pension scheme. Perhaps an apt sentiment that captures Greenland's position is that famously espoused in the film *Brokeback Mountain*: 'I just can't quit you.' There is no way of avoiding the inconvenient truth that Greenland relies overwhelmingly on Danish funds to support socio-economic development and make possible its day-to-day prosperity.

Independence for Greenland will continue to be incremental and largely piecemeal until the nation develops a self-sustaining economic base. On this foundation, Denmark can transfer further responsibilities to Greenland and the island can afford to execute all related governance duties. Obviously, the first place to start is monetising Greenland's resource bounty.

But Greenland's resource wealth is the enduring allure for Danish interest in the region. Spats have already occurred between Greenland and Denmark over rights to control (and capitalise from) Greenlandic resources. The 2013 decision to lift the ban on mining radioactive materials is evidence of simmering tensions between the two over strategic resources.[19] It was finally agreed that Greenland was the decisionmaker when it comes to the extraction of uranium from its land. However, Denmark retained the power to decide whether uranium could be exported. What good is a strategic resource wealth if one cannot sell it?

There is latent potential for Greenland to step out of Denmark's shadow. Of course, Greenland is no newcomer to shaking things up—institutionally speaking. Back in 1985, Greenland became the first territory to 'exit' the European Economic Community (EEC).[20] When enacting the Home Rule Act, Greenland struck a deal, upon exiting the EEC, to become an overseas territory associated with the EEC. This ensured free movement of peoples, duty-free market access for Greenland, and access to aid schemes. Greenland pulled a 'Brexit' before it was cool to do so.

Greenland is a force of nature in political terms, packing quite a punch for such a small power. Her track record of holding Denmark to account, promoting self-interest wherever possible, and setting a remarkable precedent for protecting indigenous culture, makes Greenland's approach to independence from Denmark even more intriguing.

The slow pace and careful approach Greenlandic leaders take on the country's quest for independence is perplexing. Is this simply the result of insecurity which stems from economic struggles? Could a cash injection from Trump's America really assist the Greenlandic quest for independence?

Greenland is a nation in transition. It has come from home rule to self-rule and waded its way to a variant of autonomy. Yet in looking for independence, Greenland is set to remain a nation in flux. Of course, in the space of only 25 years, Greenland went from a Danish colony to having its own parliament. This is rather impressive compared with the journeys of others.

Australia took over a hundred years to move from British colony in 1788 to a constitutional monarchy by 1901. For those new to Australian governance, Australia has independence from Britain, but the British Crown is still the head of state. The monarchy of the United Kingdom can dissolve (and has dissolved) the Australian government. Australia is a useful analogy when considering just what 'independence' means and looks like in action.

Greenland is not European. It is not American (yet). And it is rather far from Asia. While it is no longer a Danish colony, it is yet to entirely free itself and grasp independence. Greenland is undergoing rapid changes, physically with receding icecaps (the Danish Meteorological Institute states the island is losing the equivalent of 100 million Olympic pools of water per year) and, of course, metaphorically—in navigating its political destiny.[21]

Now, it is high time to trade some Greenlandic war stories.

4

Greenland and the World Wars

Greenland's existence was widely publicised thanks to global war, which in turn kicked off the enduring desire to 'own' it. Now, most of Greenland is uninhabitable, being an island that is 80 per cent icesheet. Nonetheless, the landmass holds vast strategic benefit.

Greenland played a starring role in both world wars and even landed a lead part in the Cold War feature. The island's experience of the world wars taught her a thing or two about great power conflict, and even more about enduring strategic competition.

Upon the outbreak of World War I (WWI) in 1914, Denmark announced it was neutral. The Nordic countries (Denmark, Sweden, and Norway) became famous for being a beacon of peace, stability, and neutrality. As great power conflict washed across Europe, the three nations maintained a unified front in their detachment and impartiality.

Much of this was down to the 'Three Kings Meeting' at which (you guessed it!) the three Nordic kings came together to consult. This occurred a mere six months into the war, and was intended to promote 'soft power' and neutrality in times of conflict. The long-standing shadow of this was of course the development of neutrality as 'a cornerstone of Nordicity'.[1]

The Danish policy of neutrality meant Greenland managed to come through WWI without entanglement. During this time Greenland remained largely a closed-off area, and folks needed permission from the Danes to step foot on the island.

But Greenland was not so lucky when Nazi Germany entered the global scene. World War II (WWII) certainly reached Greenland's shores, and it all began with the fall of Denmark in April 1940 to Germany. While there was no annexation or physical occupation of Greenland by Nazi Germany, there *was* German occupation of Denmark. This meant Greenland fell under control of an occupied Danish realm. For one man in Washington this situation presented a tantalising opportunity. That man was Henrik Kauffmann, about whom more later.

The strategic 'prize' of Greenland during WWII was its geographic location. Not necessarily in terms of what the location provided belligerents by way of bases or territorial control—but of the information or data to be gleaned from the island. Greenland was the theatre for the Weather War (1942–1944). Its location meant atmospheric data (temperature, wind, cloud) could be used to predict the weather headed for Western Europe.

In the North Atlantic, weather patterns are rather predictable, moving west to east. Want to know what the weather is like in France? Keep an eye on the weather patterns in the High North or Arctic area. The higher and further north you can go, the better the picture of what is coming your way. Precise warning data is going to give any actor an 'edge' in conflict. Indeed, much of the Greenlandic data collected was pivotal for the Allies in determining windows and timings for most major battles and landings.

During WWII, Allied weather stations popped up on Greenland, but there were also many attempts made by Germany to gain a foothold in the weather station 'race'. Even before the US formally entered the war, the US Coast Guard was active along the Greenlandic coast and her waters, chasing off Nazi intelligence missions to establish covert weather stations.

Nazi Germany did manage to construct at least two covert weather stations in the northeast area of Greenland. The US Coast Guard worked in partnership with a crack action unit, known as the Greenland Army, to rid the island of Nazis. Now, the Greenland Army was only about 15 people powered by dog-sleds. And the Nazi footprint at its weather stations often involved about six personnel. Today the Greenland Army is known as the Sirius Patrol—and still defends and monitors Greenlandic land.

With the fall of Denmark in 1940, the political status of Greenland became murky. For the Danish Ambassador to Washington, Henrik Kauffmann, however, this presented a stellar opportunity. And so, a critical chapter in Greenland's history was opened. Kauffmann believed Greenlandic security and sovereignty were going to crumble because of Nazi-occupied Denmark. Although the history books are vague on his exact motivation, a review of diplomatic cables held by the Official Historian archives of the US Department of State points to a legitimate fear on Kauffmann's part that Denmark would be unable to protect Greenland from the enemy.

The US was not the only actor that sought opportunistic gains from Greenland's murky political situation. Canada and the United Kingdom (UK) also vied for increased engagement with Greenland. Canada did establish a consulate on the island, with a view to bolstering ties with its neighbour. However, the interest of the United Kingdom was problematic for a US committed to the Monroe Doctrine.

A UK footprint in Greenland, under the guise of protecting the island from enemy control, was a non-starter for Washington. The US's Monroe Doctrine had long established that Europe was not to 'interfere' in the Western Hemisphere. Any attempts to do so, from colonisation to political intrusion, would be deemed by Washington a direct threat to American security. And so, once Washington's interest in 'supporting' the security of the Greenlandic people was voiced, the United Kingdom backed off.

Once the US formally entered WWII, and established a foothold in Greenland, further geostrategic benefits of the island were unlocked. Its position afforded somewhat of a 'stepping stone' from North America to Europe. This remains a vital link to this day. Any military general will attest that logistics win wars. The ability to re-fuel, service, and maintain aircraft and naval assets in Greenland ensured operational efficiencies for the Allies throughout the later stages of WWII.

The terms of and background to the US unlocking Greenland's strategic 'prize' are important. It is known that Greenland fell under US protection during WWII, but the context and secret negotiations to arrive at the agreement are less widely understood. Which brings us back to Henrik Kauffmann.

Kauffmann was in Washington serving as the Danish Ambassador when war erupted. Within a month of WWII breaking out, by May 1940, secret negotiations were started by Kauffmann with the US. By April 1941, he had signed an agreement with the US to hand over Greenland under a protectorate status—ushering in the era of US military bases and American forces in Greenland.

The ins and outs of how this happened made for a wild ride and unsurprisingly have already become a Hollywood hit (*The Good Traitor*). Kauffmann, as Danish Ambassador to the US, took it upon himself to negotiate the status of Greenland while Denmark was under Nazi occupation. But did he have the authority to do so? No one seemed to know at the time. Of course, once the two governors of Greenland backed Kauffmann's plan to secure Greenland as a US protectorate of sorts, it seemed that the question of authority disappeared altogether.

Kauffmann's position that he represented the legitimate plight of Greenland was certainly bolstered by the support of Greenland's governors—Eske Brun (Governor for North Greenland) and Aksel Svane (Governor for South Greenland). The unity of their position presented to the US no doubt legitimised the basis for negotiations between Greenland and the US.

Of course, vital strategic interests of Denmark were under threat in Greenland. Besides the potential for enemy occupation or annexation, the pivotal cryolite mine at Ivigtut was cause for Greenlandic concern. This in turn threatened the unity of the Danish realm. Governor Svane is on record as stating that 'more adequate defense of the mine was needed as the cryolite income is vital to the well-being of Greenland and the capture or destruction of the mine would be catastrophic'.[2]

Cryolite was crucial to the production of aluminium—used at the time for aircraft—and was therefore obviously a coveted item in wartime. The mine at Ivigtut, established in

1856, was one of the world's largest. Crucially, it was the *sole* cryolite mine operational during WWII.

Apparently, the Canadians cottoned on to the strategic risk (and unilateral benefit) of controlling the mine and planned to seize it in early April 1940. Ottawa's plan was dubbed 'Force X'—a mission to control the mine to ensure Germany could not. Whether or not Hitler had such a plan remains contested to this day. At a meeting between Canadian Prime Minister W.L. Mackenize King and US President Roosevelt, it is said that Roosevelt directly requested the Canadians to 'stay off' Greenland, for the US had grand plans to 'protect the territory's neutrality'.[3] Within the coming months, Washington opened a naval base at Grønnedal—ostensibly to protect the cryolite quarry.

These US plans to protect Greenland weren't warmly welcomed in Denmark.

On 12 April 1941, the Danish Ministry of Foreign Affairs submitted a 'definite protest' to any initiation of negotiations over Greenland with Kauffmann. According to the diplomatic cables, Kauffmann was not warranted to act on behalf of the Danish government either 'ex-officio or pursuant to special authorisation from his government'.[4] Kauffmann was exiled in Washington, and the Danish Ministry of Foreign Affairs viewed any agreements undertaken by him to be not binding at all.

Arguing that the ministry, as well as the Danish government more broadly, was not acting independently given its German occupation, Kauffmann responded in a diplomatic cable that he felt 'under the circumstances, there was, to me, no doubt but that I must, in the interests of Denmark and Greenland, take this unusual step' to seek US protection. He stated that he 'acted in a way which [he] felt to be right, after careful consideration and according to [his] best belief and the dictates of [his] conscience, fulfilling [his] allegiance to His Majesty the King'.[5] I would buy that.

Certainly, US Secretary of State Cordell Hull 'bought' Kauffmann's explanation. Hull agreed that the Danish government was very likely acting under duress in its rejection of Greenland becoming a US protectorate.[6] Hull also disregarded Denmark's view of Kauffmann and continued to formally recognise him as an authorised representative of that country.

A tit-for-tat diplomatic cable exchange endured for almost a year. This was no longer a departmental problem. It was clear there was real Danish opposition to Washington's proposed plan for Greenland. Kauffmann himself was tried in absentia in a Danish court for treason, for his part in seeking to 'give away' Greenland to the US. Then the dispute between Denmark and the US reached presidential and royal level.

On 19 April 1941, President Roosevelt sent a letter directly to Denmark's King Christian X. Roosevelt made it clear that he supported Kauffmann, the plan, and the overarching purpose behind it. He laid out the White

House's thinking on the issue, saying that there was an urgent need to protect Greenland owing to an absence of assurance that foreign forces would not 'suddenly or without warning' occupy Greenland.[7]

Roosevelt made it clear that his concerns had to do with the island being occupied by a nation other than Denmark. His solution, as he explained to King Christian, was that Washington planned to hold 'Greenland in trust for Denmark until such time as the Royal Danish Government ceases to be subjected to duress on the part of an occupying nation and full Danish control over Greenland may be restored'. Roosevelt assured the Danish king that 'no legitimate interests will be affected adversely by the action of the US in Greenland'.[8]

Some seven days later (a length of time then considered rapid), on 26 April, King Christian replied. Kauffmann had indeed lost the confidence of the king, with Christian telling Roosevelt that any agreement signed in his name by the exiled diplomat was invalid. Despite this unequivocal rejection of Kauffmann's authority to conclude any deal for Greenlandic security, Washington continued to disregard this.

Diplomatic cables of the time illustrate the panic then gripping the Danish government. The idea of facilitating the occupation of Greenlandic territory by any foreign power, even for protectorate reasons, was 'unthinkable' for Denmark.

In subsequent letters, the Danish monarch warned Washington that any continued negotiations with Kauffmann on the question of Greenland were tantamount to 'rendering [the] diplomatic contract between Denmark and the US at Washington impossible' and threatened that, in doing so, 'a very important tie would be broken'.[9]

Roosevelt basically replied 'sorry not sorry' and the US cracked on with its planning for 'saving' Greenland. Ties between the US and Denmark remained strained, and Danish vessels in American (and Philippine Islands) ports began to be requestioned by Washington.

Then on 9 April 1941, a watershed moment for Greenland occurred with the signing of a defence agreement between the US and the exiled Danish Ambassador. This authorised the US to protect Greenland. Of course, upon *whose* authorisation this was made remained clear as mud. This question, given the strategic prize of Greenland, was probably something Washington was quite happy to overlook.

The 1941 Agreement Relating to the Defense of Greenland was made public soon after it was signed.[10] The preamble stated that Greenland was cut off from the motherland and as a result the US was concerned by the 'exposed position of the Danish flag in Greenland', the plight of the Inuit population, and the threat posed to 'established public order' on the island. The agreement, using the pretext of the US Monroe Doctrine, noted that the US feared

'European territorial possessions in America may be converted into strategic centres of aggression'. Greenland was clearly the territorial possession Washington was angsty about becoming a Nazi-occupied hub of terror.

The agreement also framed the security of Greenland as 'essential to preservation of the peace and security of the American Continent'. The document clearly listed Greenland as a 'subject of vital concern' to the US. The agreement quite explicitly stated that Danish sovereignty over Greenland was fully recognised. This was caveated with a note that Denmark's capacity to exercise its powers with respect to Greenland was impeded by German occupation.

The specific content of the agreement was articulated in ten articles. Article I dealt with the sovereignty question. There was no question about it: Denmark held the title. But under Article I, the US 'accept[ed] the responsibility of assisting Greenland in the maintenance of its present status'. Reading between the lines: Nazi-free.

Article II of the agreement dealt with the rights assigned to the US by Denmark. Washington received the 'right to construct, maintain and operate such landing fields, seaplane facilities and radio and meteorological installations' as necessary. 'As necessary' was the first whiff of dubious legal wording baked into the agreement. Article III covered US rights to improve the said military installations, deepen harbours, and construct supporting infrastructure, from roads to housing. Article III also specified the US 'right to do any and all things necessary to insure the efficient operation, maintenance and protection' of its defence facilities.

Article IV somewhat pushed the envelope of the original intent of the agreement. It stipulated that the constructed facilities on Greenland would be made available to the US for activities in support of the 'common defense' of the Western Hemisphere. This was of course a clear indicator that the US plans for Greenland might not have an expiry date. Article V doubled down on the US footprint. It afforded Washington the right to use the facilities on Greenland for the period of the agreement remaining in force. The kicker? Article V held that there was no need for 'formal lease negotiations'.

Like a problematic tenant, the US was evidently digging in for the long term. Article VI restated that sovereignty over Greenland was to be retained by Denmark, but when it came to jurisdiction over military installations, areas, and personnel, the US was in charge. Of course, there are numerous scholarly legal debates about the role of jurisdiction and administration over territory and the relationship of such activities to sovereignty. Without jurisdiction over much of Greenland, did Denmark still have sovereignty? Likely, this was not a critical question of the time—after all, there was a world war going on.

Article VII of the 1941 agreement was rather boring, allowing US rights to establish postal facilities in Greenland to connect back home. Indeed, this is another act of administration, befitting a sovereign. The next two articles (VIII and IX) remain dull and unsurprising—US exemption from customs duties and taxes, and agreement to respect 'native' laws and customs, respectively.

But Article X is anything but bland. This is the section that deals with the duration of and limits on the agreement to hand Greenland over to the US for safekeeping. Simply put, there were none. This new status quo was to remain in force 'until it is agreed that the present dangers to the peace and security of the American Continent have passed'. Further, any modification or termination was to be 'subject to agreement between [the] US and Denmark'. Even then, there was a required termination notice period of 12 months.

Article X is a real punch in the guts. It is entirely a matter of perspective and interpretation when it comes to deciding if 'present danger' has passed. One party could just disagree, thus keeping the agreement in place. Should dangers have passed for good? Or for the month? Temporally, how was 'present' defined? Likewise, the peace and security of the American continent appear to be the real focus of the agreement, which seems disconnected from the primary rationale of safeguarding Greenland while Denmark and Europe sort themselves out. There wasn't even an easy escape clause.

By May 1941, Greenland (again, via Kauffmann) formally requested US assistance. The US established a consulate in Greenland and by 10 May the first US Coast Guard (USCG) cutter, *Comanche*, had set sail for the island. Four more USCG vessels would make the journey soon after. On 6 May 1941 the US Navy assumed command of USGC operations and the broader Greenland theatre. The mission was clear: protect Greenland, establish US military bases, and support the Greenlandic people.[11]

US weapons hit Greenland's shores—to defend the mine at Ivigtut—by the end of May. Weapons included a three-inch gun, eight .30-calibre machine guns, 50 rifles, and bulk ammunition.[12] Construction began on the first US base— Bluie West One—by July 1941. In 1943 the US ventured to the northwest of Greenland to establish Thule Air Base (today known as Pituffik Space Base). All in all, the US established some 13 bases throughout Greenland, and WWII saw up to 6,000 US military personnel living and working on the island. This is notable in terms of the sheer scale of the US footprint given that at the time the population of Greenland itself was less than 20,000 people.[13]

The US code for Greenland was *Bluie*. Washington had a sense of humour. Each base established on the island was either a 'Bluie West' or 'Bluie East'. Bluie West One was the US base and airstrip at Narsarsuaq. Other airfields were located at Bluie West Eight (at Søndre Strømfjord) and Bluie East Two at Ikateq.

Further bases operational between 1941 and 1945 included radio, weather, and patrol stations at Bluie East

One (Prins Christianssund), Bluie East Three (Cape Tobin), Bluie East Four (Ella Ø island), Bluie East Five (Eskimonæs), Bluie West Two (Kipisako), Bluie West Four (Teague Field), Bluie West Five (Egedesminde), Bluie West Six (Thule), Bluie West Seven (Grønnedal), and Bluie West Nine (Cruncher Island).[14] By the end of WWII there were about 30 weather stations operated by the US on Greenland.

The introduction of US forces to Greenland was mitigated in part by the public unity displayed by Kauffmann and the two governors of Greenland at the time. Both governors (Brun and Svane) worked tirelessly to urge the Greenlandic nation 'to exhibit a correct and worthy manner towards our [American] guests'.[15]

Now, the idea that Hitler had designs on Greenland is contested. Sure, the Nazis would have eyed access to strategic resources—notably cryolite—or at the very least looked to disrupt or choke off Allied access to it given its centrality to aircraft manufacturing at the time. But the geographical position of Greenland, atop the North Atlantic, made any such mission precarious at best. U-boats might have managed, but resupplying any Greenland base or sustaining any occupation would have been difficult. After all, the Germans were becoming bogged down in Europe.

Kauffmann remained fervently committed to his virtuous reasoning for the Defense Agreement. He expanded on his motivations, stating his intent was simply to 'make a contribution to the war effort through the placing of Danish territory at the disposal of the United States in the fight against the common enemy'.[16] It is hard to hate the guy. No wonder the treason charges laid against him were dropped once Denmark was liberated. He even ensured the foyer of Denmark's new embassy in Washington (built just after WWII ended) was laid with Greenlandic marble.

Kauffmann's motivation to secure Greenland from Nazi Germany's hands was on balance rather righteous, but the US government approach does somewhat reek of opportunistic action.

In practice, the defence of Greenland during WWII was very much home-grown. By mid-1941 the famous North-East Greenland Sledge Patrol had been established. This was a dog-sled patrol group tasked with observing and reporting on any encroachments onto the vast icesheet. There are accounts of one or two clashes, with Nazi scientists discovered hiding out on the northeast coast of Greenland—covertly radioing back weather data to Berlin.[17]

Comprising Inuit and Greenlandic-based Danes, the patrol group had unparalleled knowledge of the land. From exploring to surviving the icy wilderness, the Greenland Sledge Patrol was the best in the (niche) business.[18] No more than 30 men in total would come to serve in the patrol between 1941 and 1945. They became known as the Greenland Army.

The 1941 Defense Agreement was adopted (much) more formally by the Danish government upon its liberation in

May 1945. But the official record indicates that there may have been a rather large communication problem between the Danes and Washington. It began, as most problems do, with the question of money. Diplomatic cables confirm that no payment was to be drawn by the Danish government for US military basing and utilisation of Greenland during the war. One cable stated the 'Danish Government therefore hereby waive their rights in regard to any remuneration due to Denmark in virtue of Article V of the agreement of 9 April 1941, for the use made during the war of the defense areas in question'.[19] Problem was that no discussion of payment schedules, rent, or fees occurred in the drafting process of the 1941 agreement. The US ignored Denmark's 'offer' to waive rights to remuneration. But the statement nonetheless indicated something was brewing.

There was some real post-war tension between the US and Denmark over Greenland. Kauffmann, now regarded as a hero of the Danes, wrote that he 'always assumed' Washington would look to establish permanent military bases in place in Greenland. In response to this statement, the US Secretary of State agreed, saying that Greenland was 'definitely [still] within the scope of the Monroe Doctrine'.[20]

Word made its way back to Denmark that this was the position of Washington. Apparently, the Danes were 'horrified' at the idea of receiving a request for permanent bases. The thinking in Copenhagen was that, given the end of the war, the two would tear up the agreement. Then came

Washington's 1946 offer to 'buy' Greenland. The $100 million offer (in gold) was swiftly rejected.[21]

The US attempt to own Greenland drifted into history, while Washington's footprint on the island quietly persisted. But the world around Greenland was shifting. The post-WWII order was emerging, and today's rules, norms, and organisations began to take shape. This in turn impacted on Greenland. Rising from the ashes of Europe's latest war were two significant international bodies—the North Atlantic Treaty Organization (NATO) and the United Nations (UN).

The UN was established on 24 October 1945, on the heels of a conference in San Francisco. With some 50 nations in attendance, the UN Charter was signed, committing nations to the maintenance of international peace, security, and law, the protection of human rights, and the facilitation of humanitarian aid.[22] Relevant to Greenland's story was the UN focus on non-autonomous areas.

The UN shone a light on the rights of indigenous populations and promoted the end of colonisation. Autonomy was a principle of the broader UN effort. Greenland's political status was fast-tracked in many ways towards a resolution, separate from the bilateral tensions over the territory between Denmark and the US. As noted in the previous chapter, Greenland ceased to be a colony in 1953, securing equality as an integral part of the Danish realm.

The second international body that emerged from the turmoil of WWII was NATO. Indeed, Denmark was one of the original 12 founding nations to sign the North Atlantic Treaty. This was of course at odds with the long-standing Danish policy of neutrality. But Denmark joined NATO under very specific conditions, including a limitation on permanent peacetime bases, a ban on the hosting of nuclear weapons, and denial of Allied military activity on its territory without invitation.[23] Greenland remained an outlier, with Denmark allowing the US peacetime military footprint to endure as per the Defense Agreement.

Throughout the post-war period it became increasingly clear that Greenland was no longer 'isolated' politically. For Denmark, Greenland was like a feisty teenage daughter—free of innocence, curious about the wide world, and intent on forging her own path. Denmark, like any parent, had house rules and boundaries, wary of opportunistic strangers ready to woo Greenland.

The changes under way in the international system spurred by the post-war strategic order were just one of the forces shaping Greenland's outlook on the world. Greenland's population had been exposed to new ways and new technologies through hosting US forces during the war. It was the little things—pre-war, the seal-oil lamp was a fixture of Greenlandic society, but the advent of war and of US forces ushered in kerosene lamps and, later, electricity for Greenland.[24]

Of course, throughout the immediate post-WWII years, it was apparent that the US had overstayed its welcome in Greenland. At least for the Danes. Yet this was not in breach of the formalities outlined in the Defense Agreement struck with Denmark. It was a delicate tension.

Did Denmark ask for US assistance during the war? Well, it depends. Some history books are scathing of Kauffmann's treachery, while others applaud his quick wit to secure Greenland away from Nazi clutches. Perhaps the truth sits somewhere in the middle. On the balance of probability, Germany very likely had designs on Greenland. But Washington, at the time of engagement with Denmark (via Kauffmann) over Greenland's situation, was not yet a combatant in the world war. The US was most certainly in the right place at the right time, afforded an opportunistic strategic creep to securing a valuable piece of real estate. Money for jam, they say.

There was little time to ruminate on how best to reverse the US's strategic interest (and presence) in Greenland. The next global conflict was already brewing. Indeed, a new 'present danger' had emerged for Washington: the Soviet Union. This new enemy was literally one stepping stone away, a neighbour on the Arctic doorstep. With the Danes bound by a Defense Agreement that was tricky to unwind, Greenland found herself smack bang in the middle of the next big feature—the Cold War.

5

Project Iceworm

Efforts to make use of Greenland's critical strategic position are best captured by the adventures of the US during the Cold War. Have you heard about the US nuclear power reactor operating in Greenland that powered a secret underground city? Did you know the US Army built a city under the Greenland icesheet? Does Project Iceworm ring a bell? Didn't think so. Let's dig in.

Post-war, the US retained a strong strategic interest in Greenland. The Pentagon quite literally thought of Greenland as 'the world's largest stationary aircraft carrier'.[1] It was therefore hardly surprising the Danes had trouble evicting the US from the island in the post-WWII years. With the US refusing to agree that 'the threat had passed'—grounds for ceasing its military footprint on the island—Denmark was frustratingly bound by the 1941 Agreement Relating to the Defense of Greenland.

It appeared the only viable solution for the Danes was to negotiate a new agreement. The Danish prerogative was to update and align the 1941 deal to suit the contemporary context of the North Atlantic Treaty Organization (NATO) security framework of the post-war order. Of course, the mission was also to limit (where possible) US activities to specific areas in Greenland. This was an attempt to rein in Uncle Sam.

In 1951 the parties negotiated a new defence agreement for Greenland. Titled 'Defense of Greenland', this new agreement put the island front and centre in terms of the North Atlantic area. This was simple geography, of course, as Greenland sits atop the North Atlantic. The preamble of the new agreement framed the defence treaty in terms of the need for NATO to be able to access facilities in Greenland 'in defense of Greenland and the rest of the North Atlantic Treaty area'.[2] Quite clearly this agreement was not directly about the security of only Washington and Denmark, or even Greenland. Indeed, it was for the benefit of NATO.

The 1951 agreement was less about facilitating US leadership in Greenland for defensive purposes and more about having a joint US–Danish defence footprint. The two governments would work together *from* Greenland. The various articles stipulate that the US was welcome to establish or operate defence areas 'on the basis of NATO defense plans' in instances in which Demark was 'unable to establish and operate singlehanded'. Now, the Danes have traditionally (thanks to their societal interest in neutrality) spent far less on the military in terms of GDP than the US has. It is therefore intriguing to consider whether the Danish government would ever have been in a fiscal position to establish bases independently, anyway.

The 1951 agreement further ensured both national flags were to fly over defence areas, and the division of operational responsibility was to be crystal clear. A Danish military representative was to be engaged and embedded into the US facilities. While the US was allotted a range of rights to operate, maintain, and sustain military facilities in Greenland, Danish authorities retained the right to move freely in US-operated areas, and Danish sovereignty was not in dispute.

Key changes in the agreement saw the US naval station (Grønnedal) transferred to the Danish government. But US military assets retained free access. To align with the NATO-centric vision of the 1951 agreement, should Denmark have trouble maintaining the naval base, then, owing to necessity, the area would be deemed a defence area under a partnership operation with the US.

As with the 1941 agreement, the US retained the right to a tax free operation in Greenland. Of course, Washington also secured the right to fly over and navigate the territory of Greenland without restrictions. But this did not mean Denmark went wanting. Article X of the new agreement sought to ensure Greenlandic interests would trump NATO mission plans. Accordingly, the 'two governments will consult with a view to making mutually acceptable adjustments'. Of course, we know how elusive consensus can be.

The new agreement clarified the defence areas in Greenland under operation by the US. Narsarsuaq, in southern Greenland; Sondrestrom in the middle belt of Greenland; and Thule, to the high northwest of the island. Narsarsuaq and Sondrestrom closed in 1957 and 1991 respectively. Thule, today known as Pituffik Space Base, remains operational. More on Pituffik Space Base later.

But the new defence agreement did not mean the US would behave itself in Greenland upon signing in 1951. Within the parameters of the new treaty, Washington deepened and broadened its footprint in Greenland. This is in many ways an early case study of 'lawfare'—the strategic use of law or agreements to bolster national power. The US may not have directly breached the agreement, but its unique interpretation certainly facilitated some interesting projects in US defence areas in Greenland.

Let's begin with Camp Century. This military installation is located about 800 miles south from the North Pole, in the rugged Greenland expanse, and roughly 150 miles from Thule. Camp Century was not really a 'secret'; ostensibly it was always a scientific research base. Plenty of science occurred there—personnel did conduct some of the first ice-core drills allowing us to map changes in climate over thousands of years. Beamed into every American lounge in 1964 was a masterstroke of public relations—a TV special celebrating the activities under way at Camp Century.[3] The wonder and awe evoked by the human endeavour on show under the ice was enough to arouse at least some measure of public support for the unique mission.

Camp Century was an important US Army strategic mission at the time. To begin, a plateau was selected, far enough inland not to be affected by summer thaws (there is slight melt of the icecap, but the area is certainly not ice-free). Polar construction was hazardous at best, and all materials needed to be imported—everything from nails and metal sheeting to ice-cream stores. In all, over 600 tons of supplies were sledded in by convoys. It took the US Army about 70 hours for goods to trek from Thule to Camp Century.

Of course, 24-hour sunlight, extreme cold, and long days made a posting to Camp Century hard work. Nonetheless, the military construction crew delivered a system of 23 trenches. Once dug, each trench was covered with steel roofing and reinforced by pushing snow back over the top. Prefabricated buildings (made of plywood) were slid into the tunnel and assembled under the steel-ice roof. Once the interior work was completed, the tunnel was blocked with snow bricks, creating a solid wall. A door was added and an escape hatch as well, should things take a turn for the worse at one end of the tunnel.

Larger ploughs were used to cut much deeper trenches at Camp Century to house nuclear facilities. Pipes for heating and water were added, as well as sewerage lines. The construction team drilled down 120 feet into the ice to establish a well providing 10,000 gallons of fresh water daily. A nuclear power reactor brought the underground ice city to life.

Construction commenced on the underground city in June 1959 and concluded in October 1960. Upon completion, 26 tunnels had been carved beneath the Greenlandic icesheet. Camp Century was so large it incorporated over two miles of tunnels.[4] Inside the city of ice were enviable living quarters with plenty of hot water showers, an industrial kitchen, a hospital, a chapel, and a barbershop. This US military outpost beneath the ice was home to some 200 people at its peak.

To power the camp, the US Army dragged components of a portable medium reactor to the site. It was reconstructed on site and delicately filled with nuclear fuel. Known as SM-1, it operated without (publicly known) problems. A leak here or there was commonplace for the US modular reactor of the time. Even Washington's attempt to use nuclear power at the other end of the earth—Antarctica— was not without its challenges. The Antarctic nuclear reactor was forever known as 'Nukey-Poo', owing to its 'leaky' tendencies.[5]

The US was not honest about the real mission of Camp Century. It was not merely a place for scientific research—it was a 'cover' of sorts for a secret quest under way to bolster US strategic deterrence. This brings us to Project Iceworm.

Unveiled documents illuminate secret discussions in the Kennedy administration promoting Project Iceworm. It planned to deploy up to 600 Medium-Range Ballistic Missiles (MRBMs) from Greenland.[6] An MRBM has a range of between 1,000 and 3,000 kilometres. In an arms race with the Soviet Union, nuclear capabilities and deterrence capacity really mattered.

Naturally, the Soviet threat posed to mainland America was just over the Arctic horizon (the shortest distance between Russia and the US for a missile to travel). Greenland's vast and isolated territory thus assumed a pointed strategic value for Washington in the early Cold War years.

Project Iceworm, the stationing of MRBMs beneath the ice, served a dual purpose at the time. First, it promised to bolster US strategic deterrence capabilities quite significantly. Second, the Kennedy administration was actively looking for ways to raise a multilateral nuclear force within NATO. Greenland, by way of Danish NATO membership, presented a tantalising opportunity to Washington under the guise of Denmark contributing to the defence of the North Atlantic area.

Camp Century began to operate as a summer camp in 1964 and closed in 1966. It wasn't until 2024 that it returned to the international stage—with a NASA team inadvertently rediscovering the city beneath the Greenlandic icesheet. It was well known in historical and defence circles that the US

Army project had once existed, and its location was no secret. But advances in satellite technologies unearthed Camp Century in extremely precise detail. No missions have been green-lit, at least publicly, to return to Camp—yet.

Project Iceworm was a secret locked away in the Greenland icecap until 1997, when the Danish Institute of International Affairs went digging. Researchers wanted to understand just how close Greenland came to being a nuclear-weapon base during the Cold War. Beyond uncovering the depths of US nuclear activity on the island during this time, and inadvertently unveiling Project Iceworm, the study illustrated 'Denmark's difficulties in controlling the American activities in Greenland under the 1951 Defense Agreement'.[7]

Another example of the US not directly breaching the 1951 Defense Agreement but facilitating some interesting operations nonetheless, could be found at Thule Air Base. Turns out Thule was a 'staging base' for US nuclear-armed aircraft and secret reconnaissance missions.[8] It was also home to a critical piece of infrastructure for Cold War America—the Ballistic Missile Early Warning System (BMEWS). This system gave the US mainland about 15 minutes of warning before Soviet Intercontinental Ballistic Missiles (ICBMs) rained down on American cities.[9]

The public-facing element of BMEWS was used to assure the Danish government that Thule, and US defence areas in Greenland more broadly, were *defensive* in nature—not *offensive*. Danish public perceptions maintained a strongly neutral and anti-nuclear flavour through the Cold War era. It was thus crucial to find any opportunity to showcase defensive capabilities on the part of Washington as a rationale for its footprint in Greenland.

But there was no way to spin an event that occurred in 1968. A nuclear-armed US B-52 plane crash-landed near Thule. The crash site was secured quickly, but word soon spread throughout the local community and made its way back to Denmark. The US was without doubt conducting nuclear-armed overflights in Greenland. This was in utter breach of Denmark's no-nuclear-weapon position. A fierce political battle ensued between the US and Denmark.

The US position was that the 1951 Defense Agreement did not specifically ban the basing or storage of nuclear weapons. In fact, it made no reference to the nuclear question at all. Hindsight is truly a female dog.

Following the B-52 crash, the Danish government put out a statement: 'It is a well-known fact that, in agreement with the policy of the Government, no nuclear weapons are located on Danish territory. This is also true of Greenland, and there can therefore be no overflights of Greenland by aircraft carrying atomic bombs. It cannot however be excluded that American aircraft may attempt to land in Greenland in an emergency.'

Questions arose and interest was certainly piqued—Washington wondered what the Danes were smoking. Had the US breached Denmark's stringent no-nuclear-weapon stance? Well, it's complicated. The US Department of State archives provide some of the answers. Declassified cables indicate that the US simply thought that it had permission to introduce nuclear weapons to Greenland, thanks to a vague letter from Danish Prime Minister H.C. Hansen.

It all began back in November 1957. US officials at the time believed Article II of the 1951 Defense Agreement entitled Washington to certain storage rights. Records show the US sought clarification on this.[10] The US 'considered it important to determine' whether the Danes 'wished to be informed prior to introducing nuclear weapons into Greenland'.

The offending letter in question, from Prime Minister Hansen, was handed to the US Ambassador by way of answering Washington's nuclear query. It was deemed 'informal, personal, highly secret and limited to one copy each on the Danish and American side'.

The content of the letter is important: 'During your visit here some days ago you made some remarks about the possible storing of supplies of munitions of a special kind on the defense areas in Greenland. I gathered that your government did not see any problem in this matter, which in its opinion was covered by the [1951] Agreement. You did not submit any concrete plan as to such possible storing, nor did you ask questions as to the attitude of the Danish

Government to this time. I do not think that your remarks give rise to any comments from my side.'[11]

The US simply read between the lines on this one. There was no objection per se, nor any follow-up queries on the Danish side. And so, nuclear weapons flowed into Greenland. From February 1958, four aircraft bombs (nuclear or hydrogen) plus fifteen different components (to build bombs) were sent to Thule Air Base. From 1959 to 1965, it is believed up to 48 nuclear warheads were brought to the base.[12] This was all to come to light in 1995.

How did US nuclear activity in Greenland remain so closely held a secret? The official US record contains some answers, but the simple answer is that the Danes did not have a strong interest in reopening the question about defending Greenland. The 1951 agreement was best kept in place, with unfortunate incidents—like the crash—pushed to the side. Clear reasoning for this is found in a US official memo, which states: 'Greenland had more autonomy now than when [the] 1951 treaty was negotiated. In any renegotiation Greenlanders would interject themselves strongly and become a complicating factor.' Boo to national autonomy.

To smooth things over publicly, the US announced all flights armed with nuclear weapons over Greenland were to be suspended following the crash. A slight modification was made, based on Danish–US consensus, to the 1951 Defense Agreement. In terms of this, the US categorically promised not to store nuclear weapons in Greenland or fly over the island with nuclear-armed aircraft, unless explicitly afforded Danish permission.

The US and Denmark patched over the incident well enough, and no one seemed bothered to ask for clarification as to how long the US had been storing nuclear weapons in Greenland or flying nuclear-armed aircraft in Greenlandic airspace. Of course, it wasn't until the depths of the US nuclear operations in Greenland came to light in 1995 that the complete picture became clear.

After WWII, US strategy towards Greenland was much less about security for Greenland and almost entirely geared towards providing security for the American homeland *through* Greenland. But plenty happened during the Cold War era for the island. As a result, the 1951 Defense Agreement between Denmark and the US became no longer reflective of the strategic and political realities of contemporary Greenland. For starters, since its inking, Greenland had gone from being a colony to an equal part of the Danish realm.

And then the 1990s came. The fashion might have been great, but music was so-so. Of course, the Soviet Union collapsed overnight, leaving little ground for the US to argue that *any* significant threat was posed to its security requiring such an expansive posture in Greenland.

In 2004, the US came together with Denmark and the Home Rule government of Greenland to renegotiate (amend) the 1951 Defense Agreement. Known as the Igaliku amendments, the document was succinct, a mere four articles.[13]

Article I stipulated Thule Air Base was to be the sole defence area in Greenland. The flags of Denmark, Greenland, and the US would fly above it. Article II sought to clarify the NATO Status of Forces Agreement (how NATO operates in host nations) in Greenland. Article III modernised the Defense Agreement for the current political environment in Greenland. As the 1951 agreement discouraged US contact with Inuit people, this provision was formally 'revoked'.

The Igaliku amendments committed the parties to consulting and informing the local Greenlandic population about US military operations. A representative of the Home Rule government of Greenland was given a liaison position at Thule Air Base. Article IV reaffirmed that the revised 1951 Defense Agreement could be amended at any time by mutual agreement.

Geography did not change when the Cold War ended. Greenland thus remained a feature of strategic planning and defence policy for Washington. The post-Cold War world was truly a messy one. It ushered in the end of the unipolar moment for the US and welcomed the rise of multipolarism. China entered the global strategic competition, and the Russian Federation rose from the ashes of the Soviet Union.

War returned to Europe. Steve Jobs gave us the iPhone. Borders collapsed and time became compressed thanks to advances in connectivity globally. All these forces of our interconnected world have also come knocking on Greenland's door.

Greenland has survived Vikings, Nazis, and world wars. But the convergence of rising powers, resource insecurities, and a warming icecap has come to pose a threat like nothing ever known to the island. Geopolitics are reshaping Greenland as we know it.

6

Contemporary Geopolitics: Greenlandic Edition

There is something truly mystical and daunting about the Arctic arena, in which Greenland exists. Stories throughout history of human endeavour in the Arctic against all odds have been handed down for generations in many countries. International exploration and efforts to conquer the vast icy extremes have been celebrated throughout the years. As this chapter explores, the ingredients for international competition, and indeed conflict, exist in the Arctic arena. Converging geopolitical pressures as well as global resource insecurities have renewed the competition (well, at least the perception of competition) to 'own' Greenland. However, to date, the region has largely avoided tensions reaching breaking point. Cooperation, not conflict, has predominantly characterised the post-Cold War Arctic.

New actors are entering the Arctic arena, including a country whose name begins with 'C'. Now, Canada is already an Arctic nation. And it's not Cabo Verde, Cambodia,

Cameroon, the Cayman Islands, Central African Republic, Chad, the Channel Islands, Chile, Colombia, Comoros, Cook Islands, Congo, Costa Rica, Côte d'Ivoire, Croatia, Cuba, Curaçao, Cyprus, or the Czech Republic.

The idea of a 'rush' for the Arctic stems from the resource wealth of the region. Both living and non-living resources are dwindling elsewhere on the globe. But this is where facts get murky and fiction blossoms. Reminiscent of the 'great game' dash to the north to secure resource bounty, there has been plenty of chatter recently about the militarisation of the Arctic.

The tale of a 'new' Cold War in the Arctic certainly sells newspapers and garners internet clicks (feeding advertisers a fat lunch). This 'new' Cold War has everything in it: from Arctic military bunkers and bases befitting any James Bond feature film, to crack army units on sleds. Of course, its main belligerents also happen to be Mother Russia and the US. Add in a dash of Chinese expansionism and an imperial quest to conquer the Arctic frontier, and you certainly have a best-seller.

But it is high time for a dose of reality. The Arctic region is quite collaborative, and cooperation features predominantly throughout the region and between stakeholders. The area has tended to remain on the sidelines of global war, although it was used as a formidable logistical theatre during WWII. But no missiles (thankfully) flew between Arctic states during the Cold War. Plenty of false alarms, diligently checked by military officers, did feature thanks to the early warning radars that both the Soviet Union and the US had erected in the Arctic theatre.

Even contemporary conflicts beyond the Arctic, like the Russia–Ukraine War, have remained outside the polar theatre. To be fair, some diplomatic and collaborative mechanisms that exist in the Arctic region initially 'froze out' Moscow from their activities, but no shots have been fired in the Arctic. The notion of military confrontation or a looming Arctic war is an unserious strategic narrative for the High North.

Of course, cool terms like 'hybrid war' or 'grey-zone activities' also tend to feature in contemporary Arctic geopolitical analysis. Here, folks are onto something. As the previous chapter explored, the US footprint in Greenland is permissible by way of the 1951 Defense of Greenland Agreement struck between the Danes and Washington. However, this legal document is prone to acts of interpretation on the part of its signatories—what is known as 'lawfare'. This has caused problems. One side's assessment of what constitutes a 'threat' is often quite different from the other's. And any agreement that requires consensus to enact any change or undertake modifications, no matter how legitimate they might be, is precariously placed to deliver on the national interest. The national interest of whom? Lawfare is about using legal tools, agreements, language, or processes to further the position of a state—often in the search for power.

Lawfare can often make possible hybrid war and grey-zone activities. It certainly has done so in the Arctic. International law at sea is promoted by all Arctic parties, and while the US is yet to ratify the United Nations Convention on the Law of the Sea (UNCLOS), it still views UNCLOS as customary international law.[1] International law is a mecca for lawfare practitioners. Under the guise of international law, states undertake activities or policies in the Arctic which aren't necessary best practice.

For example, Russia has interpreted an article of UNCLOS (Article 234 to be precise) to place an entire Arctic transit route off limits. Moscow uses lawfare to argue the route is affected by ice and therefore obliges Russia to enact certain protocols for environmental and safety reasons (as outlined by Article 234). The protocol in question means international access to and use of the Arctic route are curtailed entirely. Pay a handsome fee, submit the necessary paperwork, and Russia might agree to your bid to use what are (arguably) international waters.

Lawfare in the Arctic has progressed by leaps and bounds thanks to advances in technologies and capabilities which allow humans to push the boundaries of the polar environment. Dual-use purpose is a concept that has arisen in the past decade or so to characterise most research or scientific missions in the Arctic. Researchers have tools and technologies today that have clear military-security applications. From sonar and submarines to drones and satellites, the Arctic theatre is full of capabilities that have research use. But their military-security utility is undeniable.

This is an uncomfortable reality for a region that promotes global collaboration and cooperation in scientific research, climate change monitoring, and capacity building for the region's indigenous peoples. Nonetheless, lawfare has ushered in both hybrid and grey-zone warfare campaigns to the Arctic. Hybrid warfare covers activities that blend various streams of effort to upset an adversary. A hybrid war campaign might see a combination of economic pressure and political or information operations targeted at a domestic population. This kind of war is about integrating conventional and non-conventional means to achieve state objectives.

'Grey-zone' warfare picks up on the (unhelpful) distinction between times of peace and times of war, and utterly blurs the line between the two. It used to be the case that war was declared, by letter or radio, with terms of engagement clearly set down. Peace involved a treaty, or handshake, followed by epic celebrations in the street. But in the 'grey zone' there are no clear intentions, nor clarification of actions undertaken. An absence of shots being fired is no longer proof of peace: war can rage in silence.

Whether hybrid or 'grey-zone' in nature, *competition* is alive and well in the Arctic. To explore geopolitical competition in the Arctic—remember, this is still far short of conflict—it is time to get to know the 'players' engaged and the 'prize' at stake. But, first, let's begin with a picture. Below is an illustration that captures the centrality of Greenland (that light landmass with the label 'Greenland') to the transatlantic and Arctic strategic theatres.

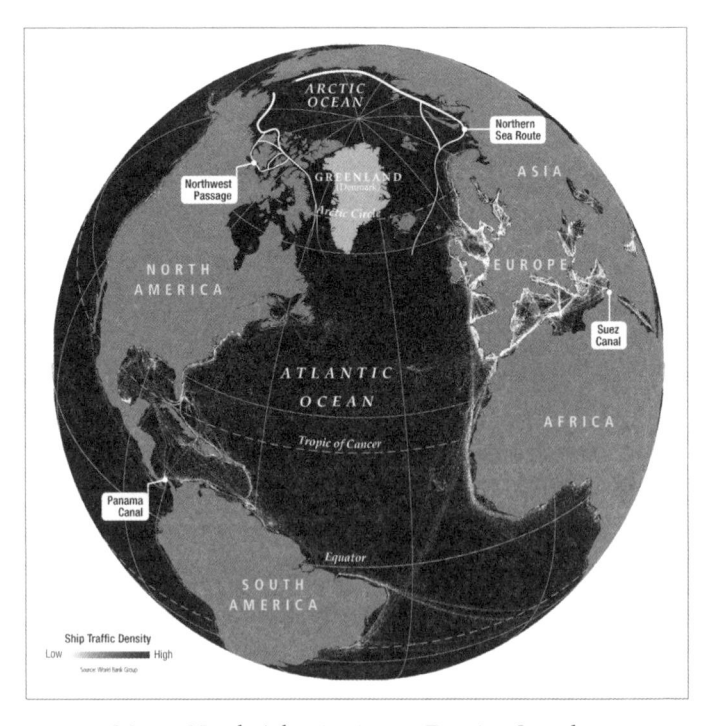

Map 2: North Atlantic view. © Damien Saunder.

In many ways, Greenland is the ultimate prize. For North America, Greenland's strategic position, by virtue of geography, makes her a very important 'buffer'. The US's enduring strategic competitor—Moscow—would have to come through (or, rather, over) Greenland to target American homes or cross a strait (sorry, Alaska). Greenland's geographic position also makes it one side of a major choke point of sorts that could control the flow of goods between Europe and Asia—particularly as the Arctic trade routes open up and global transportation shifts north. More on this later.

Further Arctic prizes are best characterised in terms of living or non-living resources. It's quite self-explanatory really. Living resources include Arctic Ocean fish stocks, and diverse mammal and bird life. And non-living resources are hydrocarbons (oil and natural gas) and minerals. For circumpolar indigenous communities—of which there are about 40 different ethnic groups above the Arctic Circle—living resources are critical to sustainable development goals and basic livelihood. While both pools of resources draw significant geopolitical interest, most resources are to be found in undisputed territories. The vast majority of non-living resources sit well within the seabed or landmass of Arctic states and aren't under dispute.

A small non-living resource bounty does lie beneath the seabed of the North Pole region in the middle of the Arctic Ocean. However, even the 'race' for this is paced and well above board. The three claimants to the seabed area of the North Pole (Russia, Canada, and Denmark—by way of Greenland) are following international law to the letter and are awaiting the outcome of their scientifically informed applications to the dispute body at the UN known as the Commission on the Limits of the Continental Shelf (CLCS).

A potential clash, however, may be brewing on the living-resource prize front. This pertains to the Central Arctic Ocean Fisheries Agreement (CAOFA). Coming into force in 2021, and involving Arctic states and non-Arctic states like China, an agreement was struck to ban commercial fishing in the Central Arctic Ocean for a period of 16 years. This covered the High Seas zone of the Arctic Ocean—in legal terms, the area of ocean in which signatories of UNCLOS are afforded freedoms. Now, CAOFA is not permanent, and any signatory after 16 years can simply object to any extension. Looking at Beijing's fisheries activities at the other end of the earth, in the Antarctic Ocean, one does question how long China will restrain its immense commercial fishing appetite.

The Arctic prize seems tantalising, but much of it is already claimed. Now, who is who in the Arctic 'zoo'? There are typically three groups of 'players' when it comes to the Arctic arena. Stakeholders, interested parties, power-hungry states: there are many ways to define nations with strategic interest in the Arctic. Each can be sorted in terms of proximity to the Arctic; for example, territory above the Arctic Circle makes a nation an Arctic-8 state. For a narrower measure, states with frontage on the Arctic Ocean are considered the most 'Arctic' and therefore are dubbed the Arctic-5. A third 'basket' of Arctic stakeholders are generally labelled 'non-Arctic' ones. Non-Arctic nations are those external actors (usually a long way from the Arctic) elbowing for a place at the Arctic table.

If this was high school, the Arctic-5 would be the varsity athletes. The Russian Federation, the US, Canada, the Kingdom of Denmark (by way of Greenland … you see the issue), and Norway are the epic Arctic-5. All five nations have territory reaching into the Arctic Ocean. These are pure Arctic nations. All (bar the US officially) use the legal tool of UNCLOS to secure various maritime territorial claims in the Arctic Ocean. Offshore resources are watched closely, and most of the Arctic-5 have bolstered their Arctic Ocean approaches with military outposts. Some have spent sustainably more than others in doing so—looking at you, Russia.

The Kingdom of Denmark, by way of Greenland, is in the Arctic-5. Greenland is the only Arctic component of the kingdom. Most areas of Arctic cooperation are within the Greenlandic jurisdiction of duties, from environmental security to the protection of indigenous rights. The region's sole governance forum—the Arctic Council—is not mandated to discuss issues of defence or military security. Cultural and environmental issues are the principal lines of effort for the Council, and these fall neatly in Greenland's policy wheelhouse. Thus the need for Denmark to claim a seat at the high table when it comes to the Arctic is therefore rather perplexing.

An additional three states (Finland, Sweden, and Iceland) sit with the Arctic-5 for lunch. Together they form the Arctic-8. Finland, Sweden, and Iceland are simply cool by association. And they have territory above the Arctic Circle. As Map 2 shows, Iceland scrapes through just barely thanks to its tiny Grimsey Island. The Arctic-8 hold permanent seats on the Arctic Council.

The Arctic Council is essentially the region's management body, of sorts. It is the only formal intergovernmental organisation for the Arctic, geared at facilitating adequate and collaborative governance for the region.[2] Established in 1996, it has successfully developed three binding agreements between the Arctic-8: cooperation on search and rescue in the Arctic, marine protection protocols for oil spills, and a commitment to scientific research collaboration.

Then there's the rest of the class. They aren't too special or noteworthy in the Arctic space. These states are keen to be seen, but are also just happy to be invited. The rest of the class only become a problem when a critical mass develops among them. Excessive non-Arctic interest in the small Arctic region has the potential to cause problems. Think: parents are away, and you throw a house party, but the invitation goes viral. Logistical nightmare, maybe. Security problem, absolutely.

Armed with knowledge of the Arctic 'prizes' and 'players', we can now consider the geopolitical forces that shape the Arctic security environment.

The first is strategic competition. Throughout history, power has shifted and changed hands in the international system. That this happens is utterly unsurprising. Our current arc of history is characterised by strategic competition between the US and China. Sea power, control of the oceans, and freedom of navigation more broadly are key features of this specific competition.

The Arctic is squarely in the crosshairs of both actors. For Beijing, the Arctic waterways are waiting to be conquered. Presence is power, and China has clearly signalled its intent to operate naval vessels in the Arctic Ocean by way of deployments. Beijing is also outproducing the US on most shipbuilding metrics, so the future Arctic already looks congested. For the US, the Arctic is Washington's backyard, and it does not intend to welcome a squatter.

A second geopolitical force shaping the Arctic security environment is 'Globalisation 2.0'. Here, new trade routes or global corridors for transportation are emerging thanks to the opening Arctic. The melting icecap makes much of the Northeast Passage (NEP) navigable during the Arctic summer. The NEP is also known as the Northern Sea Route (NSR); however, the NSR is merely a section of the NEP. It connects Asia to Europe and cuts the transit time by 40 per cent compared with the traditional Suez Canal route. The NSR component of the NEP hugs the Russian Arctic coast. As discussed, Moscow has artfully used lawfare to militarise and secure this corridor. This places the NEP/NSR largely off bounds for the West. This doesn't seem to bother China.

The other utilised Arctic transit route is the Northwest Passage (NWP), linking Asia to Europe via the North American coast. This is far more complex to navigate and, with heavier ice coverage, not a viable transport corridor in the short to medium term. The third route, the trans-polar route, cuts through the Central Arctic Ocean atop the North Pole. This is somewhat of a pipe dream, even in the long term, should the icecap ever thin enough to afford ease of passage for icebreakers, but there is little evidence this would occur before 2080. The sheer isolation of the route, compounded by operational challenges like 24-hour darkness, would surely make this passage utterly uncompetitive to service, insure and respond to in event of emergency.

Any opening Arctic trade route is by no means safer than existing ones. 'Fast ice' makes the route treacherous and somewhat risky. Now, risk is an expensive thing in the global transport game, and insurers tend to place a premium on Arctic transportation. This is of course passed on to the customer, negating any fiscal gains from the shorter route.

The third geopolitical force shaping the Arctic security environment is that of resource insecurity. A global crunch—across both living and non-living resources—has forced many non-Arctic states to gaze north. Critical minerals have emerged as a significant drawcard for Arctic newcomers. Traditional oil and gas hunger makes Arctic offshore deposits viable. However, commercial factors must be considered first. To make a barrel of Arctic oil competitive on the global energy market, Brent Crude would need to be around $200/barrel. This would allow investors to see a return on their money. Without any incentive to invest in new offshore oil and gas projects in the Arctic, it is unlikely any 'race' to unlock the deposits will eventuate.

Finally, a fourth geopolitical force shaping the Arctic security environment is climate change. The Arctic region is one of the world's most affected zones when it comes to global warming. Military bases throughout the Arctic-5 territories are crumbling as permafrost melts and the Arctic ground becomes unstable. Wildfires are a common feature of Arctic summers now, too. Climate change also draws non-Arctic state interest towards the region. Asian states (India and China primarily) are investing heavily in climate research and tools to predict future weather patterns. More and more scientific research missions are being deployed to the Arctic to monitor climate change. Of course, as any hybrid and grey-zone warfare expert would know, these scientific missions have dual-use purposes. One state's scientific mission is another's intelligence mission.

Greenland, 80 per cent of which is covered by ice, is significantly affected by climate change. It isn't just the physical melt of Greenland's icesheet that affects the nation. Yes, infrastructure becomes unstable and costly to redevelop. But it's the unseen changes that really undermine Greenland's economic and societal security.

Warming waters around Greenland and changing salinity thanks to ice-calving and icesheet melts affect the Arctic marine ecosystem. When fisheries and marine mammals move, key food sources disappear for the Arctic peoples. One of the reasons why the Inuit may have outlasted the Vikings back in the 1400s was the hunting practices and knowledge of the Greenlandic ecosystem possessed by the Inuit. But with climate change these hunting grounds and, along with them, centuries of 'living off the land' are under threat. Greenlandic people are needing to adapt.

In response to contemporary geopolitical forces, the government of Greenland has issued two key documents. The Greenland Mineral Strategy was released in 2020.[3] It replaced the Oil and Mineral Strategy (2014–2018), which failed to be realised because the international mineral market did not 'explode' as had been assumed. The new strategy has simplified the exploration and licensing process in Greenland and kept sustainable development at the centre. It reveals an interest in promoting small-scale resource development projects to enable the local community to become involved, and also to support the establishment of a local industry for Greenland. Less investment *in* Greenland, more investment *for* Greenland.

The second document is much more consequential for Arctic geopolitics. The government of Greenland released its first foreign, security, and defence policy in 2024. Titled *Greenland in the World: Northing about Us without Us*, the policy is all-encompassing but is primarily an Arctic strategy.[4] Given the island's geographical location, this makes a lot of sense. The document outlines the Greenlandic need to 'adapt' to new strategic realities lapping on its shores. From sharpening climate changes and new conflicts in Europe spurred by Russia's invasion of Ukraine in 2022, to the Covid-19 pandemic, Greenland concedes it is not immune to security shifts in the world.

Of course, the document clarified Greenland's independence of sorts in the context of its relationship with the Danish realm over Arctic affairs. While Denmark identifies as an Arctic power and is treated as such in most Arctic fora, Denmark itself does not technically fall above the Arctic Circle, and its 'Arctic-ness' stems simply from its ties with Greenland.

Greenland's foreign, security, and defence policy has made it clear that its long-term goal remains 'independence' and, accordingly, it seeks to 'engage with the world'. The document stipulates that all foreign relations are to be 'based on the premise that Greenland and the Greenlandic people constitute an independent people and nation'. The island's relationship with Denmark is referred to in terms of its being 'part of the Kingdom of Denmark', and in this respect the document is an attempt to carve out a space for Greenland within the broader security and defence policy of the Danish kingdom. Of course, tensions remain, with Denmark retaining responsibility (and power) over Greenland's foreign, security, and defence affairs.

Of interest in the Greenlandic foreign, defence, and security strategy is the use of climate insecurity to argue that the territorial waters of Greenland need to be extended from 3 to 12 nautical miles off the coast. This is done under the guise of increasing 'environmental regulations' and to 'strengthen the control of potential resources' in Greenland's territorial Arctic waters. In practice, this would be a huge change for the Arctic, potentially resulting in a profound shift in Arctic geopolitics.

Currently under consideration at the UN CLCS is the three-way overlapping claim to the seabed of the North Pole section of the Arctic Ocean. As discussed earlier, it is Denmark, not Greenland, which lodged an application for the extended continental shelf and associated rights to the riches of the Arctic Ocean seabed and sea column. But these resource riches in the continental shelf, and up under the North Pole, would actually belong to Greenland, not Denmark. One wonders how kindly the Danes might take to losing their Arctic resource bounty.

Greenland's 2024 foreign, defence, and security strategy captures the nation's intent to strengthen 'peace through dialogue'. This is quite different from the US foreign policy of today—the 'peace through strength' posture. It is not clear which approach is prevailing in the broader Arctic geopolitical climate.

Greenland's 2024 Arctic policy states that Arctic peace is required for sustainable development. Given that sustainable development is the key to securing viable independence from Denmark, peace in the Arctic is a pretty high priority for Greenland. The government of Greenland goes further to offer its assistance in the Arctic security realm. The 2024 policy notes the Greenlandic ambition to monitor the Greenland–Iceland–United Kingdom (GIUK) Gap. This Cold War-era seabed checkpoint was once home to NATO sonar and submarine tracking capability, which monitored Soviet submarines as they entered the North Atlantic. However, Greenland stipulated it would do so in a surveillance capacity only, as, per the 2024 strategy, 'it will not take any measures that would contribute to an arms race in the Arctic'.

In many ways, Greenland has been a passenger in the Arctic strategic theatre. But that seemed to shift with the 2024 strategy, which essentially announced that Arctic security threats would be dealt with, or at least confronted, not by Denmark but by Greenland. These are grand plans, and respectable ones at that, but the resourcing question remains to be realised. How exactly does Greenland plan to deter and defend in the Arctic? How can a small nation ensure international norms and laws are upheld by larger, more powerful non-Arctic powers?

Luckily, at least today, there is no great game, no race for riches, nor any battle to 'own' the Arctic. Most resources are well within delineated and established exclusive economic zones (EEZs) in the Arctic. And players have largely abided by the rules till now.

But, as the saying goes, time and tide wait for no man. And in the Arctic, change is certainly afoot. Of course, it would be premature and somewhat off base to argue such change is going to result in confrontation or conflict. The Arctic is frigid, isolated and unforgiving. Just try living there. Greenland has long navigated the challenges, threats, and risks posed by its Arctic environment. Harnessing the opportunities presented in the Arctic and exploiting them to sustain itself economically is a delicate task for Greenland. But it is an important one: after all, self-sufficiency breeds independence.

Geopolitical races aside, Greenland's central security challenge appears to be its evolving relationship with Denmark. All politics are well and truly local.

7

All Politics Are Local

Lost in the background of the 'Trump to annex Greenland' narrative is the Greenlandic people's enduring quest to 'own' their island. Unknown to many, there is a considered, organic, local process under way to secure Greenland's sovereignty. And it begins at home.

Full disclosure, dear reader: this author has no horse in this race. I am neither Danish nor Greenlandic (and I am not American). What follows is a chapter that simply canvasses the facts on the ground and examines the domestic discourse related to the Greenlandic independence movement.

As explored in previous pages, Greenland has been on quite some journey. From Danish colony to country, to self-governing autonomous territory of the Danish realm. It all sounds very progressive and positive, right? Well, yes and no. It remains a fact of life that Greenland continues to be heavily reliant on Denmark for social services and economic support.

Denmark still manages Greenland's monetary policy as well as its foreign, security, and defence relationships and policies. Those versed in the ins and outs of domestic violence perpetrators would have to recognise some similarities here. More on this later.

No one, certainly not Denmark, is claiming Greenland is stuck. Indeed, the 2009 Self-Government Act underscored and celebrated the Greenlandic people as a nation entitled to 'the right of self-determination, with the option of independence'. The 2009 Act came into being on the back of a 2008 referendum in which 75 per cent of the Greenlandic people voted for greater autonomy from Denmark.

There is no denying that there is (a) an established interest in Greenland to reduce its reliance on Denmark; and (b) an agreement of sorts between the two for Greenland to 'leave' when it is ready. Therefore, the real question becomes not *if* Greenland will secure independence, but *when*.

Political parties in the Greenland parliament stated publicly that the nation is 'irreversibly on its way to independence, [but] this process requires not only political stability, but also national unity'.[1] This is very telling. It speaks to the fact that the 'when' of Greenland's independence quest is more of a process issue than a question of choice.

International focus on the Greenland independence movement tends to frame the topic as a battle of wills between Denmark and Greenland. In reality, at least thus far, Denmark is resigned to a possible future in which Greenland gains independence.

Let's look at the polls. These are thrown around often, but not necessarily correctly understood. A poll of Greenlanders in 2017 found most wanted independence from Denmark only if it came with zero economic deterioration.[2] The Greenlandic variant of having one's cake and eating it too.

This 2017 poll found 44 per cent would support independence only if it meant life would stay the same. Twelve per cent of respondents would happily accept the 'cost' of leaving Denmark, to secure independence. Twenty-seven per cent polled did not want full independence from Denmark—instead, they sought any solution in which self-government is enhanced. Of interest, this percentage has increased from 18 per cent in 2002. More Greenlanders in 2017 supported a mechanism of expanded self-governance. Curiously, those Greenlanders gunning for independence, no matter the cost, have also grown in size. In 2002, only 6 per cent supported independence 'no matter the cost', but by 2012 this number had *doubled*.

Almost a decade later, in 2025, polls indicated that the 'costs' of leaving Denmark still weigh on the Greenlandic mind. Nonetheless, securing independence is still very much an overall mission. One 2025 poll found that if Greenlanders had to pick, 55 per cent would select Danish citizenship, 8 per cent would opt for US citizenship, and (more tellingly) 37 per cent simply 'don't know' which one they'd pick.[3] The poll found that 45 per cent of respondents would want independence 'only if' there was no impact on lifestyle; only 18 per cent supported 'unconditional' independence; whereas 9 per cent didn't want independence, and 7 per cent stated they 'don't know'.

Now for some context: this was a poll of 497 Greenlanders over the age of 18, so this represents the views of less than 1 per cent of the total Greenlandic population (about 57,000). Statistically significant?

One wonders if the Greenlandic people are considering the crux of the issue—the difference between sovereignty on one hand and independence on the other. Sovereignty means 'supreme' authority to govern, make laws, and control internal *and* external affairs without interference. This is about ultimate power.

There is also an element of legitimacy in the concept of sovereignty, especially when a state seeks to operate on the global stage. This has of course been something at the edges of Greenland's independence push—as global interest in the Arctic shines a spotlight on the region, Greenland can step out of Danish shadows. However, as part of the Danish realm, it has limited freedoms to do so.

On the other hand, independence is simply about being free from external control or influence. It is the ability to exist, operate, and function autonomously. Given the reach of Denmark into Greenland's foreign, security, and defence sectors, we certainly can't class Greenland as fully independent.

A state can be sovereign but not fully independent if it's still influenced by external powers (say a healthy block of funding each year). Likewise, an autonomous territory of a realm can have *some* independence but lack sovereignty.

Are sovereignty and independence the same thing? No. Does it matter? Only the Greenlandic people can truly answer that. But surely investigating this tension for Greenland is of principal concern? There is little (public) evidence that the sovereignty versus independence debate has been held in Greenland to date.

A cursory view of Greenland's domestic political discourse points to more of an interest in securing 'equality' with Denmark. Ensuring the right to be a master of its own destiny, securing independence in even more areas—like foreign, security, and defence affairs. Greenland is not necessarily on a quest for full sovereignty, it seems.

This points to an uncomfortable reality: Greenland will never truly be entirely independent, either. Instead, the notion of independence for Greenland is more of a continuum. Should this be the case, then it would make sense to clarify such a position. If only to rebuff or wave off any future attempts to 'own' Greenland. You can't buy what's not for sale.

Therefore, Greenland's quest for independence from Denmark is best framed as an enduring process. In 2003,

Greenland's Commission on Self-Government dug into the political futures of the island. A report was produced that offered six avenues available to Greenland: full independence, union, a free association agreement, federation, an enhanced state of self-governance, or integration with another state. It had the makings of a 'choose your own adventure' book. Independence garnered the most support.

In 2016, the Greenland parliament established a Constitutional Commission to get a sense of just what independence would look like. How would independence work in practice? The Constitutional Commission published its final report in 2023. It included a draft constitution for Greenland.[4]

Some legal eagles would point out that the Danish Constitution makes it impossible for Greenland to have its own constitution. This is probably why progress on the 'draft' constitution has been slow, for there is a delicate dance under way. Denmark's 2009 Act on Greenland Self-Government does state that the autonomous territory is 'free to initiate a preparatory constitutional process'. Greenland's parliament has yet to debate the draft constitution. That would trigger the need for a national referendum and formal steps toward secession.

The Constitutional Commission's report makes for interesting reading. The executive summary describes a process of inquiry that was as much haphazard as it was complicated. The commission took six years to undertake the work, many of its members changed during this time, and iterative changes to the commission's terms of reference occurred. In the end, the terms of reference essentially required the commission to consider how changes to Greenland's status would 'fit into a Greenlandic legal framework'. These are the issues at the heart of any constitution.

The report's background section is (necessarily) scathing. It speaks about Denmark 'steering the process' of Greenland's status after the creation of the United Nations in 1945. Denmark is accused of 'incorporating' Greenland in 1953 into the Kingdom of Denmark, and then swiftly promulgating the Danish Constitution, which tied Greenland to the realm.

The report argues the Greenlandic people didn't get any right to vote on the process, and specifically that they were not 'offered alternatives' to incorporation—like a free association agreement. In effect, Greenland became an 'equal' part of the Kingdom of Denmark. But, the commission says, incorporating Greenland into Denmark was also to get the Danes off the UN shit list. In 1954, the UN applauded Denmark for its work to end its colonising behaviours. But, the report states, 'large parts of the colonial structure and logic continued intact'. The commission frames the journey to the 2009 Act on Self-Government as one of 'mature decolonisation'.

Greenland's draft constitution begins: 'the Greenlandic people are and always shall be self-determining'. Discussion of the island's history and heritage is framed in terms of their contribution to Greenland's wealth. Which, as the report states, 'is our responsibility'. The ecosystem and Greenland's natural state are a central theme of the draft constitution, which notes: 'we live from and with nature, and this is an inalienable principle in order to ensure a sustainable society for our time'. This of course is at odds with the existence of sectors like mining, and the vast exploitation of Greenlandic mineral wealth. It is a problem for any self-sufficient economic vision given the resources Greenland possesses.

The draft constitution supports the idea of Greenland remaining a community with collective rights, in which 'common ownership of our entire land, sea and all resources is inalienable'. Ownership specifically covers 'land, sea and all resources'. The draft includes practical aspects of the workings of the constitution, covering the institution of a threefold separation of powers (legislative, executive, and judicial). Citizenship is afforded to those born in Greenland, or to children if a parent has citizenship. Greenlandic is confirmed as the official language. No reference is made to Danish.

There are rights and freedoms aplenty in the draft constitution. Freedom of expression, hunting rights, freedom to gather, are all covered. According to the draft, the death penalty 'shall never be introduced' and the nation won't allow slave labour. Operationally three committees would feature in the Greenland parliament—a finance committee, foreign policy committee, and a law committee.

Section VII of the draft constitution is compelling. Focused on foreign policy and international relations, it speaks volumes about the ways in which Greenland wants the world to see it. Both duties would be controlled by the Greenland parliament. International relations are defined by the constitution as including 'fish stocks, health cooperation, climate policy, research cooperation, educational cooperation, cultural cooperation, and transport policy'.

But the door to external cooperation in these sectors is left wide open. If the Greenland government wishes to do so, it can 'transfer powers or competences' to other states or intergovernmental organisations. However, the draft constitution requires parliament to have a three-quarters majority in favour to do so. A national referendum among the Greenlandic people must then follow, before any transfer of power or competency occurs.

In a discussion section of the commission's report, more light is shed on the thinking behind items that feature in the draft constitution. Of interest is the discussion on the merits of free association. A UN resolution (1541) from 1960 is cited with regard to the establishment of free associations in the Pacific region.

The report notes that powers can be successfully transferred to a 'greater or lesser extent' to another state in areas of competence where the freely associated state might otherwise lack 'capacity and/or resources'. It goes on to say that free association also often includes economic transactions between two parties. Is this a stark reference to Greenlandic representatives feeling they are *already* operating in a free association with Denmark?

There is plenty of focus in the document on the transfer of power. Commission members had reason for doing so, of course. The draft constitution concludes that the 'Greenlandic Parliament may never transfer powers to another state or intergovernmental organisation without [Greenland] still hav[ing] the opportunity to exercise influence on decisions that affect Greenland and the Greenlandic people in the areas where power is transferred'. What this in effect means is a transfer (maybe 'loan' is a better term) of power with baked-in assurances of Greenlandic sovereignty.

The draft constitution does not close the door to formal alliances or, say, foreign military footprints. It states, 'Greenland may, in relation to diplomatic or similar matters, enter into agreements with other countries on special rules and laws.' However, any agreement tied to defence or security affairs must be anchored in 'cooperation' with other states, and only undertaken where Greenland does 'not have capacity' to maintain the 'appropriate level of defence and security for the territory, society and its citizens'. In any case, the draft clearly states that the territory of Greenland is 'indivisible'.

Overall, the draft constitution is not great news for the Danish Crown. There is zero reference to the role of the Kingdom of Denmark in Greenland's political make-up. Likewise, there is no clear definition of several terms in the document. What constitutes a foreign, defence, or security affair or issue? Definitions of military-security and notions of what constitutes a security threat have no doubt changed over the decades.

In recent years there has been a proliferation of advances in technology and dual-use capabilities (things that have both a military and a scientific purpose). This is certainly the case in the Arctic arena, one characterised by scientific collaboration between states, which often opens the door to dual-use capabilities entering the theatre. China's research vessel mapping climate shifts may also be using satellite technology to sharpen its surveillance of North America, for example. What constitutes a military-security issue therefore becomes pretty much entirely a matter of perspective. One man's research weather balloon is another man's intelligence asset.

The draft constitution's commitment to remaining open to cooperation with other states on matters of defence and security provides somewhat of a glimmer of hope for Denmark. After all, Greenland is hugely (or bigly) important to Denmark for its own strategic purposes. While the US might see Greenland as a valuable piece of real estate for its own defensive and strategic purposes, Denmark looks to Greenland to bolster its own strategic *reputation*.

The reason for this is that Denmark is rather tardy in its defence commitments. NATO's own estimates state that Denmark spent only 1.65 per cent of its GDP on defence in 2023.[5] It had hovered around 1.3 per cent of GDP in prior years. There are plans to get to 2 per cent of GDP, hopefully sooner than the current plan to get there by 2030. This makes Greenland more important to Denmark. The latter gets a bit of a 'free pass' because of Greenland's strategic value to NATO.

Greenland's strategic importance to NATO stems from its geographic position: it is critical for monitoring Russian military activities. Russia is of course NATO's reason for being. NATO objectives are supported by the US Pituffik Space Base on Greenland, not to mention all the super-secret stuff there which churns out information crucial to NATO deterrence planning. As part of the Danish realm, Greenland is kind of offered up on a plate as evidence of Denmark's contribution to the alliance.

Greenland's draft constitution is a promising document. But progress beyond this has been lacklustre. Of course, the exercise was not about establishing whether Greenland has the right to secede from Denmark. It has long been established that this right exists, and it is even included in the 2009 Act. The commission's work was about clarifying the options and terms of Greenlandic independence in practice.

The lack of clarity over terms used will no doubt be a future problem for Greenland. This was a missed opportunity, particularly given Greenland's current challenges with 'lawfare' and the opaqueness around duties in its relationship with Denmark today. For example, the 2009 Act does shift many domestic duties to Greenland for autonomous management. Economic and trade affairs are clearly under Greenland's jurisdiction, while foreign affairs, defence, and security issues are controlled by Denmark. But some two decades later, what constitutes a security issue or how economic affairs are defined is simply no longer the same.

Nor are political issues easy to delineate or classify. Chinese investment in, say, Greenlandic mines is surely a domestic economic affair. Right? Not necessarily. Say the mine in question is for strategic minerals and the US has pressured Denmark to block the deal. Denmark could easily declare that foreign ownership of strategic sectors like mining constitutes a grave security threat to the realm, and Greenland would have to agree.

But it is not just the functionality of the Denmark–Greenland relationship in practice that presents issues for Greenlandic independence. The prospect of independence is weakened because of the consistent push to link Greenland's path to independence with the need to 'unlock' its resource wealth.

Certainly, self-sufficiency is going to be key for Greenland to gain independence. Being able to operate without relying on the Danes to run Greenlandic social services (healthcare and education) or to provide the annual block grant of funding is a precondition of independence. But focusing on Greenland's mineral wealth (both onshore and offshore) is not the answer.

It is assumed in the 2009 Act that minerals will ensure Greenland's future. The Act states that any funds generated by resource development in Greenland would result in the reduction of the Danish block fund by 50 per cent of Greenland's total resource earnings. This process would only start once Greenland pocketed earnings of 75 million Danish krone (about $11 million). The block grant would continue to reduce until it was zero, thus ending the annual payment from Denmark. Resource earnings from Greenland's mineral wealth would then be split between Denmark and Greenland.

While the Act (on Self-Governance) established that the resources in question do belong to Greenland, and that Greenland holds the right to extraction and would offer a payment schedule to satisfy the Danes, it presupposed quite a bit. Namely, that Greenland's mineral wealth is coveted. We know the Arctic 'gold rush' and race to secure dwindling global resources is mostly a beat-up geared at selling papers. Commercial realities paint a rather different picture. For the current state of Greenland's mineral sector is elementary at best. While many permits for exploration have been granted over the past decade or so, as of 2025, only two mines are in operation.

Here, the US has endeavoured to help Greenland. The US has supported mapping and aerial hyperspectral surveying of Greenland with a view to bolstering mineral exploration data. You can't attract foreign investment if you don't know how big the resource bounty truly is, let alone where it is. This long-held partnership is of course background information missed by contemporary tales of Washington's interest in Greenland.

In 2019, the US and Greenland agreed on a framework for cooperation on mineral sector governance.[6] The MoU was signed by Greenland's Minister for Mineral Resources and Labor Erik Jensen. This is important because Jensen was also the Greenlandic parliamentarian who famously quipped 'We are open for business, but not for sale' in response to the first Trump administration's interest in Greenland.[7] Jensen was also the leader of Siumut—Greenland's largest political party (and staunch supporter of the independence movement).

Back to the mineral MoU. It formed the basis of an agreement to survey about 3,000 square kilometres of southwest Greenland. The aim was to 'maximize opportunities to develop key energy and mineral sectors' and to support Greenland in its quest to 'attract diverse and private investment to achieve its own energy and mineral resource security goals'. Jensen noted the MoU was 'the beginning of a new phase' of the US–Greenlandic relationship and a 'mutual commitment to cooperation and development of this sector'.

Greenland's mineral wealth has also been eyed by the European Union (EU). In March 2025, the EU opened its first Arctic office in downtown Nuuk. Mineral wealth was clearly the drawcard. Building upon the EU's 2023 Strategic Partnership on Sustainable Raw Materials Value Chains with Greenland, the president of the EU Commission paid a visit to the island—citing the goal of helping Greenland develop 'huge potential' in the critical mineral space. By the EU's own count, some 25 of the 34 critical raw materials identified as strategically important for the EU are said to be found in Greenland.[8]

External interest in Greenland's mineral wealth gives off a whiff of opportunism. Of course, should Greenland come online as a resource pit for all, one could argue it would be the world's first 'Inuit Petro-State'.[9] No doubt this is an undesirable long-term goal for the Greenlandic people. Indeed, the idea of Greenland as a future resource superpower is also somewhat misleading. The basic commercial requirements for Greenlandic resources (specifically oil and natural gas) to be competitive on the international market—that is, *desirable* from an investment standpoint—are not in place.

Some of the challenges that Greenland's resource competitiveness faces are basically insurmountable. Greenland's location and proximity to markets are great, but extraction in the polar environment, not least from an island of ice-covered rock, is costly. In energy security terms, demand might be there, but Greenland—a polar island where production and the overall supply chain are determined by the weather—has a serious supply problem. Energy security is like a coin, of which demand and supply are the two, indivisible sides.

Further environmental issues make the long-term viability of Greenlandic mineral exports questionable. Some 80 per cent of the island is covered in ice. Extraction costs are immense, and the absence of industrialised towns also makes exploitation difficult. Infrastructure, from sealed roads to ports, must be built. Then there's the personnel requirement. Where is the workforce to come from for such labour-intensive extractive work? And if you plan to fly them in, where will they reside? How will the community function and operate?

Beyond the evident challenges related to realising Greenland's resource ambitions, there's also the pesky issue of proving where it is in the first place. Often cited are the results of the US Geological Survey (USGS). The USGS uses a 'probabilistic' approach—assessing geological areas and arriving at a probability of whether they might contain undiscovered oil or gas. Nothing is certain or fixed. A 2019

USGS mission estimated that the offshore east Greenland area contains approximately 31,400 million barrels (equivalent) of oil and 148 trillion cubic feet of natural gas.[10]

Even once they are located, monetising the resources to Greenland's benefit is difficult. The numbers have even been crunched—to end the Danish block grant, no less than 24 (large) resource projects would have to operate and make profits.[11] Today, only two projects could pass as large-scale (Isua and Kvanefjeld). However, Isua (an iron-ore mine) has been idle since the Chinese operator was stripped of its licence back in 2021.

Unpacking the Greenland–Denmark Dynamic

Beyond the public commitments (on both the Greenlandic and Danish sides) to modernise and move forward their relationship, theirs is a union fraught with a harrowing history. From institutionalised abuse to high unemployment and inadequate education services in Greenland, the Danes still have plenty to make amends for. Two key efforts in this space involve Danish reparations for historical injustices inflicted on the Greenlandic people.

The first is referred to as 'The Experiment', also termed the 'Little Danes Experiment'. In 1951, 22 Inuit children were removed from their homes and placed with Danish families.[12] It was a very public programme—even the Queen of Denmark spent time with the children—and was sold as

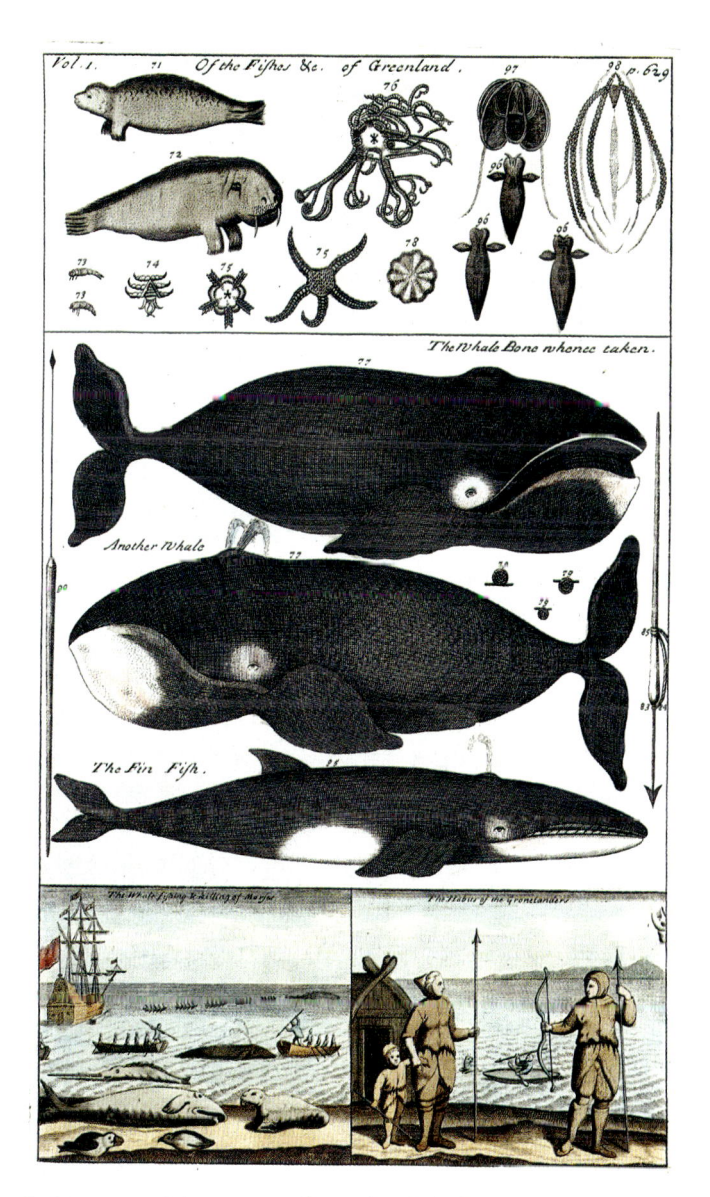

Indigenous fish, mammals and whale-hunters, Greenland, eighteenth century. Alamy images.

Hans Poulsen Egede (1686–1758) a Danish-Norwegian Lutheran priest who launched a successful mission among the Inuit of Greenland and funded Greenland's capital Godthåb, now known as Nuuk. Wikipedia Commons.

Memorial stone to Erik the Red's landing in Qassiarsuk, Greenland, in 982. Alamy images.

Whaling fleet off Greenland in the eighteenth century, after a work by Sieuwert van der Meulen. Alamy images.

Statue of Erik the Red, Greenland. Alamy images.

A Coast Guard combat cutter detonates demolition charges to clear a path through pack ice along Greenland's east coast. This operation was part of the effort to locate and disrupt a Nazi base during World War II. Alamy images.

US coastguardsmen and soldiers advance over the ice in skirmish formation toward a small island off Greenland, where the Germans had secretly established a radio station and weather reporting base. Alamy images.

The capture of twelve German soldiers by US forces was a key victory in securing Greenland from Axis control during World War II. Alamy images.

Colonel Bernt Balchen (right), of the US Air Force, whose exploratory work led to the construction of Thule Air Base, Greenland, points out the route to be followed by a Scandinavian Airlines System plane on its inaugural flight from Los Angeles to Copenhagen via Thule, Greenland. Balchen will be aboard, along with Georg Unger Vetleson (left) of SAS and Danish Ambassador Henrik de Kauffmann (centre), 18 November 1952. Alamy images.

Search for H-bombs after an American B-52 crashes in Greenland's North Star Bay, 7 miles from the USAF base at Thule, 23 January 1968. Alamy images.

Queen Ingrid of Denmark (centre) aboard an old Greenlander *Umiak* (a boat traditionally used by Inuit women) during a state visit, 8 August 1968. Alamy images.

North Star Bay with Thule Air Base in the foreground, 2006. Alamy images.

Piles of rusting fuel drums from the abandoned World War II US Airforce Base, Bluie East Two, Ikateq, Greenland.

The motorcade carrying US Vice President J.D. Vance, Second Lady Usha Vance, National Security advisor Mike Waltz and Energy Secretary Chris Wright motors across the tundra on a visit to Pituffik Space Base, Greenland, 28 March 2025. Handout/White House Photo/Alamy Live News.

a national scheme to raise 'model' Greenlanders. In 2022, the (six) living survivors were awarded fiscal damages.

A second effort involves restitution for Denmark's involuntary contraception policies for young Inuit girls in the 1960s and 1970s.[13] In 2024, 143 Inuit women sued Denmark for fitting them with intrauterine contraceptive devices (also known as coil spirals). In all, Denmark has admitted over 4,500 women and girls (as much as half of the fertile women in Greenland at the time) were implanted with the devices.[14] At the time, Greenland's population was growing rapidly, and this cost Denmark money.

The point of rehashing such atrocities is to question why on earth Greenland *stays* in the Danish realm. Of course, the practicalities of independence as explored in previous pages shape Greenland's behaviour here. But what if there's more at play? The Greenland–Denmark relationship in many ways is illustrative of two complex psychological phenomena: the Stockholm syndrome and coercive control (often found in cases of domestic violence).

Stockholm syndrome is the feeling of fondness, or trust, that a victim often develops towards a 'captor'. Some sufferers empathise and identify with their captor or abuser. Often this can be a result of the victim acquiescing in the control exercised by their captor, ultimately as a method of surviving. Being liked or tolerated by an abuser, the logic follows, affords favour and may improve future outcomes. Stockholm syndrome also sees victims often 'downplaying' the situation and working to rationalise their captor's or abuser's actions.

The syndrome often results in overdependent behaviours. The victim may further strengthen dependencies so as to survive. Gifts or small acts of grace are met with overwhelming gratefulness on the victim's part. Often, victims will seek reason in the perspective of their abuser or captor. Even after release or freedom, a victim may still relate to or harbour positive feelings for their abuser or captor.

We could view the slowing pace in Greenland to put the draft constitution through the next steps of parliamentary approval, and then national referendum, somewhat as Stockholm syndrome behaviour. Remaining in 'limbo', in terms of the progress of Greenland's independence quest, is in many ways acquiescing in Denmark's control as a method of surviving. Of course, overdependency is an obvious overlap.

The other psychological phenomenon, coercive control, often found in cases of domestic violence, sees patterns of abuse shaping a relationship. While a slow process, over time it takes away freedom and independence. Coercive control can be emotional, physical, spiritual, cultural, financial, or even a combination of these. Actions include controlling where someone goes or whom they speak to, as well as monitoring or overseeing daily activity, and controlling needs like finances and access to or provision of healthcare, education, and food.

Coercive control can also manifest as threatening statements and 'if you, I will' type of ultimatums. Often, victims don't even know they are being abused. Non-physical abuse is often not registered as abuse, and some people might feel the (abusive) behaviour is a normal part of their relationship (especially if onlookers don't say something).

There are several coercive control aspects evident in the Greenland–Denmark relationship. The financial block payment is emblematic of Denmark's continuing power over Greenland. Greenland's healthcare and education systems are provided by (and controlled by) Denmark. Greenland is unable to enter foreign or defence discussions without Danish approval.

Or is Greenland a strategic mastermind? Does it know full well its relative weak strategic position and thus its true bargaining choices? Could we argue Greenland 'free-rides' on Denmark? It might be the case that the island nation plays off the US against Denmark simply to bolster its own negotiating position. After all, following the renewed US interest to 'buy' Greenland, the Danish government rushed in and promised to inject at least $1.5 billion into the island.[15]

When it comes to 'playing off' two interested parties, there are some lessons to be learnt from the South Pacific experience. These small nations, who have ties with both China and the US, are often presented with a 'choice' between the two. The Solomon Islands, for example, actively hedges its bets between two external powers—tying its economic future to China while maintaining defence ties with the US's 'deputy sheriff' Australia. Everyone is frustrated, no one trusts the other, and strategic tension is rife. Honesty is the most prudent policy.

To consider the outlook for the Greenland–Denmark relationship, it is worth boring ourselves with a pinch of dull academic theory. (I promise, it is worth it.) International relations scholar Hedley Bull (side note: an epic Aussie export) spent quite some time digging into the concept of sovereignty. And it is sovereignty which is at the heart of the Greenlandic cause today.

Sovereignty, as previously discussed, means having power and control over territory and not being subject to the control or interference of others. Bull argues that states spend too much time assuming sovereignty rather than *asserting* it.[16] This captures quite neatly what Greenland is up to. The draft constitution focuses on 'indivisible' rights and sovereignty for the island, but very little is said about asserting sovereignty. If Greenland lacks the practical tools—from industrial capacity, to workforce, to the fiscal capability to stand independent—to assert its sovereignty, then arguably it isn't sovereign at all.

For Bull, sovereignty is the state's ability to exercise supreme authority within its territory (internal sovereignty), while having independence from external control (external sovereignty). Greenland's autonomous territory status within the Kingdom of Denmark complicates the sovereignty picture. While Greenland exercises significant internal sovereignty, Denmark retains authority over foreign policy, defence, and monetary policy, thereby undermining full external sovereignty. Bull would conclude Greenland has no supremacy, as Denmark holds considerable power.

To exercise sovereignty, a state requires economic self-sufficiency. Greenland's heavy reliance on Danish subsidies (still over half of the public budget), and the inability to date to diversify economic pools (fishing dominates exports), weaken Greenland's internal sovereignty score. This dependency creates a 'subordinate' relationship, incompatible with full internal sovereignty.

Greenland's external sovereignty is constrained, by way of the 2009 Act, but it is evolving. Bull would argue that achieving external sovereignty hinges on international recognition post-referendum, should the draft constitution progress to parliamentary debate and beyond. Till then, without fiscal independence, Greenland's government remains subordinate to Denmark. Greenland possesses partial internal sovereignty but lacks external sovereignty.

Understanding whether it is independence or sovereignty that Greenland is seeking is a circle that needs to be squared. Meanwhile, the Greenland–Denmark relationship endures. It is difficult to capture the true essence of the relationship today. In many ways, it is a saga of rivalry and conflict hidden deep beneath a mask of unity, equality, and progress.

Of course, modern Danes aren't cool with being reminded of their colonising past. This makes the block grant payment even more complex. Is it payment for progress? For silence? For subservience? Or is it guilt money? Admittedly the answer depends entirely on perspective. Both Greenland and Denmark would have differing thoughts on the matter.

The broader geopolitical construct in which the Greenland–Denmark relationship exists is also increasingly complicated. The Arctic has become a global focus, if not looming flashpoint. Greenland is well and truly in the thick of it, just in terms of proximity to the new 'great game' alone. Yet the Arctic geopolitical climate can also offer insights into Greenland's capacity to act independently in the region.

Denmark's appetite to cede sovereignty to Greenland on Arctic affairs will also be tested increasingly. For example, according to the 2009 Act, Greenland can 'negotiate and conclude international law agreements' with foreign states and international organisations—unless Denmark is directly involved, in which case the Danes take the reins.

The Arctic is squarely a Greenlandic affair. By way of basic geography, Greenland is more Arctic than Denmark. Consequently, one can plainly see how Arctic issues fall under internal affairs for Greenland. But great power conflict in the Arctic could undoubtedly also threaten the 'unity of the realm' and thus invite Danish action.

One avenue 'out' of the Danish realm is China. Greenland could partner with Beijing and bank some serious coin. But we've already seen how such engagement has been flagged by Denmark as a security or defence issue and promptly blocked. To be fair, Greenland has also worked to secure its own territory from 'the China threat'. From revoking mining licences and exploration permits, to rejecting Chinese-backed bids to buy strategic infrastructure like an airport, Greenland has been on the ball. Of course, one should never write off the Chinese Communist Party (CCP). Indeed, China's foray back into Greenland might not be merely the work of the CCP–Nuuk may in fact opt to work with Beijing to unlock its economic self-sufficiency. Scenarios of this sort are explored in depth in the final chapter.

Greenlandic independence is best described as a train between stations. Signals from the newly (2025) elected Greenlandic parliament (Inatsisartut) are promising but still lack gusto. While all the main parties in Greenland support independence, the 2025 election winners, the Democrats, are eyeing a long-term approach towards independence.[17] Greenland's new coalition government brings together four of the five parties in the Inatsisartut. The fifth party, Naleraq, remains outside the coalition due to its belief that the independence process should be hastened significantly.

It would appear that both Greenland and Denmark prefer to retain the status quo in their relationship. Neither seems intent on rocking the boat. Therefore, the march towards independence is going to be nothing but incremental. But the choreography of the relationship is something to behold. Platitudes of unity and celebration of their national solidarity and camaraderie are always flowing, at least in the international news media scene.

One wonders if Greenland has any real incentive to seek independence. It appears as if the island is facing two choices right now: stability or chaos. Stability offers predictability, security, and structure. Stability minimises risk and, for Greenland, enables long-term planning and incremental progress towards the independence goal. But stability can also breed complacency and undermine long-term motivation to 'break free' from Denmark.

Chaos, on the other hand, embodies uncertainty and unknown possibilities. Upheaval of course is uncomfortable, but to grow and change, Greenland will need to take risks. For now, Greenland appears to prioritise stability. Nothing changes the fact that Greenland has established its right and ability to seek independence from the Kingdom of Denmark. It has a pathway for doing so set out in an agreement with Denmark. What remains unclear is what the threshold is for Greenland to pull the trigger and break away. The draft constitution seemed promising, but little has evolved since then.

When (not if) Greenland does gain independence, there will no doubt be trade-offs. But already, these trade-offs aren't necessarily welcomed—just look at the results of various polls that support independence without any compromises to the standard of living. Independence may not be progressing swiftly, but it would be disingenuous to blame Trump, the US, or Denmark for this situation. Greenland's agency is not without moment.

How on earth did Greenland find itself in this position? As noted, Greenland's Constitution Commission was quick to lay the blame at the feet of Denmark for pushing through Greenland's shift from Danish colony to Danish country. But could Greenland have *done* something in the intervening years? Other states have managed to exit Denmark's clutches quite undramatically—just look at Iceland.

Like Greenland, Iceland found itself an isolated island when Nazi Germany occupied Denmark in April 1940. Iceland was also part of a union with Denmark up till this time. Upon the occupation of Denmark, Iceland began its move towards independence. Iceland held a referendum, and on 17 June 1944 it became an independent republic.

Now this isn't an exercise in direct comparison—but nor are we comparing apples and oranges. Both Iceland and Greenland have a Danish link, are isolated islands, have small populations (even Iceland is only roughly 390,000 strong), and similar GDP per capita. Clearly, contemporary economic and geopolitical challenges are delaying Greenland's progress on the independence front. By virtue of opportunity, Iceland had a smoother transition. While Iceland's sovereignty is a settled reality, Greenland's remains aspirational, with significant barriers to achieving the independence Iceland secured decades ago.

Greenland's aspirations were tempered with some cold water by Prime Minister Jens-Frederik Nielsen, who announced in March 2025, 'We don't want independence tomorrow, we want a good foundation.'[18] A short statement, but it provides clarity, nonetheless.

Remember, Greenlandic independence is like a train stuck between two stations. It is on its way, surely. But many looking at Greenland's future continue to miss the wood for the trees. A March 2025 poll found 85 per cent of Greenlanders do not wish to become part of the US.[19] This statistic was promptly tweeted and published globally. Commentary missed the fact that the question itself was framed as a binary proposition: 'Do you want Greenland to leave Denmark and become part of the US instead?'

This same poll also threw up some fascinating data about Greenlandic views of Trump. It found 45 per cent of Greenlanders viewed Trump's interest in the island as a threat, while 43 per cent said Trump's interest is an opportunity and 13 per cent were undecided. Almost equal to the Trump-wary were the Trump-curious.

Breaking free from the 'Danish teat' will require at least in part the opening of Greenland's resource treasure chest. Unless there is a global resurgence in interest for seal ivory or seal pelts, Greenland has little else export-wise to offer. But this presents a deeply ethical problem for Greenlandic people. As articulated in the draft constitution, the environment is culturally significant for the Greenlandic people.

Sustainable development of Greenland's resource bounty is possible, but it is going to have at least a minor environmental impact on the land and seas. This challenge is best expressed by Greenlandic MP Josef Motzfeldt: 'We have to choose on the one hand between unrestricted exploitation of our resources in order to gain more independence, and on the other hand the protection of our nature, which is so dear to us in order to maintain our cultural heritage.'[20] An incremental independence approach seems fitting considering this impossible tension.

Greenland is the James Blunt of geopolitics and international security. It has one or two 'big hits'—its resource wealth and geography. And it returns every decade or so to the stage. Both are complex, have a history, hold war wounds, and can (arguably) monetise their position. Like James Blunt, there's nothing to categorically dislike about Greenland. Nonetheless, there is that niggling feeling whenever it rears its head.

Now, take out your copy of *The Art of the Deal*, and let's enter Trump land.

8

The Art of a (Green) Deal

US President Donald J. Trump has not tried to hide his intention to 'own' Greenland. In as many words he has stated the 'United States of America feels that the ownership and control of Greenland is an absolute necessity'.[1] There is method to the madness, and understanding the strategic thinking behind this present quest to 'own' Greenland is the focus of this chapter.

Coffee urns were primed and ready to go on 27 March 2025 at Nuuk's Hotel Hans Egede. Named after the Lutheran clergyman discussed earlier, Hotel Hans Egede also happens to be the only air-conditioned conference facility in all of Greenland. The venue's entire conference floor had been booked by White House 'staff' a few days earlier. Something was clearly brewing. But in the end, no coffee flowed.

The White House abruptly cancelled a planned social visit, which was to see Second Lady of the US (SLOTUS) Usha Vance win the hearts and minds of the Greenlandic people. The 'glam squad' and advisors planned to hunker down in the Hans Egede conference facilities and get to work. SLOTUS's mission included attending a dog-sled race. It was all very proper. The only problem was that the Nuuk community wasn't having a bar of it.

SLOTUS was to be joined by (then) National Security Advisor Mike Waltz and Energy Secretary Chris Wright. It is unclear whether Mike and Chris possess a deep interest in dog-sled racing. Nonetheless, Washington's security and energy interests were clearly at play.

The mission plan was essentially to shake hands, put a friendly face to the administration, drag a Vice President (VP) kid along, promote bilateral ties, and drop by the US Pituffik Space Base on the way home. Now, on paper the plan was not controversial. The timing, however, was.

Greenland's national election had only just occurred in the weeks prior to the planned visit. The Greenland government was in caretaker mode. The optics of any powerful state, let alone one so publicly airing its annexationist intent, touring another country undergoing a domestic transfer of power are distasteful at best; detrimental to the broader cause at worst.

Local backlash was evident in protest activity in Nuuk prior to the visit. Realising the indelicate nature of this community immersion mission, not least the appalling timing, the White House changed the plan. The booking at Hotel Hans Egede was nixed, with the hefty deposit likely unrefundable. VP J.D. Vance was hauled into the plan and, along with a small entourage, paid a quick visit to US servicemen and women at the Pituffik Space Base. No dogsled race was witnessed, no visit to Nuuk, and no VP kid tagged along.

This public relations disaster was quickly forgotten. Instead, the press lapped up further assertive comments delivered by the Trump administration at the Pituffik Space Base visit. An entire chapter on Trump's Greenland rhetoric may seem odious, depending, of course, on your politics. But it is important to map the development of Trump's Greenland interest so that we can adequately consider the trajectory it may yet take.

The Trump administration's focus on the Arctic region was underscored by a historic address by Secretary of State Mike Pompeo at the 2019 Arctic Council ministerial hosted by Finland.[2] This May 2019 address sent shock waves through the Arctic geopolitical community and among onlookers far afield. Trump's Secretary of State lamented the loss of US leadership and sovereignty in the Arctic 'great game'. He squarely laid the finger of blame on China and Russia, but more so on China's 'creep' into the Arctic arena. This was shocking because the Arctic Council, as most well know, is not mandated to discuss or debate issues of military-security affairs. While it is the sole governance forum for the Arctic, stakeholders keep military-security or strategic issues (and any reference to them) at the door.

Pompeo's address went so far as to reject fellow Arctic power Canada's activity in and claims to the Northwest Passage. Bemused audience members could not believe the boldness, the inappropriateness and the abject lack of due regard for the governance forum. Then came the moment to draw up the meeting declaration. For the first and only time in history, the Arctic Council ministerial meeting ended without issuing a declaration. Instead, a joint ministerial statement was made. Apparently, the US delegation refused to sign any document that used the words 'climate' or 'climate change' in reference to the Arctic.

The May 2019 Arctic Council meeting should have rung alarm bells and, not least, pointed to a clearly different mode of operation for Washington in the Arctic. US interest in the theatre fell quiet until later in that year.

Trump's own preoccupation with Greenland first reared its head (publicly) in early August 2019. There were rumbles in the press of a private dinner conversation between Trump and his aides in which the idea of owning Greenland was raised. Of course, it wasn't taken too seriously until Trump took to what was then called Twitter. This variant of presidential communication soon enough became integral to the conduct of business for the White House. Social media would facilitate US leadership and signal policy intent, while staffers and communication specialists were all but kneecapped.

Through social media, on 21 August, the US president cancelled a scheduled meeting with the Danish prime minister. Trump shared: 'Denmark is a very special country with incredible people, but based on Prime Minister Mette Frederiksen's comments, that she would have no interest in discussing the purchase of Greenland, I will be postponing our meeting scheduled in two weeks for another time … The Prime Minister was able to save a great deal of expense and effort for both the United States and Denmark by being so direct. I thank her for that and look forward to rescheduling sometime in the future.'[3]

Beyond this shocking method of conducting US statecraft—apparently the Danes found out about the cancellation via social media—there was now some clarity on Trump's Greenland interest. Evidently, the 'purchase' of Greenland was a very serious policy for the administration. Policy intent had also been promulgated at home, with the US government starting to enact presidential intent. In a letter to the US Foreign Relations Committee, the State Department outlined the US's strategic interests in 'enhancing political, economic, and commercial relationships across the Arctic region'.[4] It further advised Congress's Foreign Relations Committee of the plan to 'protect essential equities in Greenland while developing deeper relationships with Greenlandic officials and society'.

The document confirmed the rumours in Washington that Trump would double down on his Greenlandic position and announce a new permanent presence on the island. Serving as 'an effective platform to advance US interests in Greenland', a US consulate would be reopened in Nuuk. The US had previously had a consular presence on the island from 1940 to 1953.

Meanwhile, the public spat over Trump's Danish visit intensified with the Danish prime minister labelling the US president's idea of annexing Greenland as 'absurd'. Trump stated he thought the Danish prime minister's response was 'nasty', pointing out that all 'she had to do is say, no, we wouldn't be interested'.[5]

Presidential feelings were evidently hurt. Trump did, however, make a relatively correct point in that the US acquisition of Greenland had been 'something that's been discussed for many years'. Beyond stating his affection for the fact that President Truman had also had the same bright idea regarding Greenland, Trump underscored the notion that he was offering to help Denmark. Relieving Denmark of Greenland, for Trump, was a no-brainer business deal, 'because Denmark is losing $700 million a year with it. It doesn't do them any good.'[6]

Manners appear to matter to Trump quite deeply—in that he was more offended by the way in which the Danes responded to his 'offer' than by the answer he got. Trump reiterated the point that he would have respected a Danish response of 'no, we'd rather not do that' or 'we'd rather not talk about it' but was disheartened (probably also offended) to instead be told 'what an absurd idea that is'.[7]

Just one day after Trump's public cancellation of his trip to Copenhagen, on 22 August, he took to Twitter once again to smack Denmark. This time, he took aim at their contributions to NATO, noting 'for the record, Denmark is only at 1.35% of GDP for NATO spending. They are a wealthy country and should be at 2%.'[8]

That very same day Secretary of State Mike Pompeo was expressing appreciation for Denmark's cooperation as an ally in the Arctic region. Even the Danes commended the relationship and 'discussed strengthening cooperation' between the US and 'the Kingdom of Denmark—including Greenland—in the Arctic'.[9] It was clearly business as usual for the Trump administration to pursue an ongoing game of 'good cop, bad cop'.

Despite the unease, Denmark gave the tick of approval for the US to reopen its Greenlandic consulate, following the visit blow-up. As per the 2009 Act, all foreign policy decisions are retained under the remit of Denmark. If the Danes had wanted to escalate this bilateral social media slinging match, they certainly could have. Of course, denying a consulate request would have resulted in more of a headache for Copenhagen than anything—the Kingdom of Denmark has far less leverage than the US.

Trump added a little fuel to the fire by soon after tweeting an image of a mammoth gold Trump Tower consuming the streetscape of a Greenlandic town, coupled with the words 'I promise not to do this to Greenland'.[10] For some, this was indicative of just how comical the intention really was—Trump was not serious. But for others, this tongue-in-cheek brashness was the epitome of the man they knew. Trump has a wicked sense of humour.

Other countries appeared to be playing at the seams of the US–Greenland–Denmark drama. A classic case of hybrid warfare was even unleashed by an unknown actor (looking at you Moscow … or Beijing … or Tehran). A letter, looking very real on an official letterhead, started to make the rounds. It purported to be confirmation that Greenland would come under the US umbrella should Washington support (and pay for) a referendum to do so. The letter was signed by Greenland's foreign minister and addressed to US Senator Tom Cotton (known to be in the Trump inner circle).[11] Now, this all seemed and looked quite real. The intention was likely to kick off chaos and unease in Greenland and Denmark, and seed disinformation about the long-standing independence process under way on the island.

The Danes had certainly taken note of Trump's eye on Greenland. For the first time ever, the Danish Defence Intelligence Service (known as the FE) placed Greenland at the heart of its national security planning. The FE's annual threat assessment (released in November 2019) opened with an entire chapter dedicated to great power competition in the Arctic. As we know, Denmark is only an Arctic player thanks to the Greenlandic aspect of its realm.[12]

Then there was the 2019 NATO Summit held in London in December. After about three months of slinging shots and causing foreign policy headaches, Trump sat down with the Danes. Denmark had taken the opportunity to announce a large increase in its defence spending, with a substantial amount earmarked for the Arctic.

By 2020, Trump's Greenlandic quest appeared to have made inroads—at least on the ground, and not merely on social media. Indeed, US Ambassador to Denmark Carla Sands racked up more visits to Nuuk while posted to Denmark than any other sitting US ambassador.

In July 2020, almost one year on from the 'Copenhagen crisis' which had played out on Twitter, US Secretary of State Pompeo arrived in Denmark. But it was all about Greenlandic business. The US announced the reopened consulate in Greenland was going well, as was the $12 million aid package it had just provided to the island. Publicly, the hefty aid package was to help with economic development and education services. However, the package also included what was termed 'US specialist consultancy work'.[13] Moving right along.

Pompeo so much as confirmed the *real* mission of his Danish visit. Upon leaving Copenhagen, all the Secretary of State could talk about was Greenland. He gushed, 'it's a new day for the United States and Greenland … Reopening the

U.S. consulate in Nuuk reinvigorates an American presence that was dormant for far too long.'[14]

By October 2020, seeking to 'unlock the great potential for partnerships and future initiatives to deepen and strengthen the relationship between the United States and Greenland', the Common Plan for US–Greenland Cooperation was agreed. It covered plans to enhance bilateral trade and investment cooperation, including the establishment of an economic policy dialogue. The plan made provision for a senior development advisor to be stationed in Greenland. Of course, there was a key focus on minerals and resources in the plan. A priority was to strengthen Greenland's technical and vocational training in the mining sector. The US Peace Corps was to launch a volunteer placement programme for teaching English in Greenlandic secondary schools.

Several other initiatives between US and Greenlandic authorities were also agreed to.[15] As per the Common Plan for US–Greenland Cooperation, further diplomatic notes were issued, including a joint declaration on improved cooperation specific to Thule Air Base (Pituffik Space Base today). The joint declaration affirmed that the base 'is central to securing this fundamental cooperation now and into the future'. There was a commitment to 'increase the benefits to the people of Greenland'.[16]

Back in Washington, the bureaucracy was busy churning out Greenlandic policy. In December 2020 an 'Arctic

Education Alliance' was announced, targeted at cultivating partnerships between universities and organisations in the US and Greenland. The focus was on supporting sustainable tourism, hospitality, and land and fisheries management.

A State Department spokesperson underscored Washington's desire for 'deeper security, deeper economic and deeper people-to-people ties between the United States, Greenland, and the Kingdom of Denmark'. The State Department even framed the aid funding package to the government of Greenland as one that would 'jumpstart [a] new beginning—this rebirth, if you will—of our engagement in Greenland'.[17]

The Trump administration's interest in Greenland was also spurred by factors from beyond the White House. Rare earths in Greenland presented Washington with a nice future resource base. The US was no longer the world's top rare earths producer, as China had taken that position. Under Trump there was a focus on regaining this lost ground. Then there was the global security picture. During the first Trump administration, the US withdrew from the Intermediate Nuclear Forces (INF) Treaty.[18] Now, the INF Treaty basically was an agreement between Moscow and Washington not to develop missiles with ranges above 500 kilometres. Plenty of finger-pointing either way saw both sides suspect the other was breaching the agreement. As examined earlier, Greenland's position is rather perfect for establishing early warning systems for these missiles as well as for hosting second-strike facilities for the US to hit Russia.

Then there was China. During the first Trump administration, Beijing made plenty of noise about its foray into the Arctic. In 2018 it even made public an official Arctic policy.[19] This country was not an Arctic-rim player, let alone an obvious stakeholder by virtue of proximity to the region. The advent of China's Arctic policy also introduced into the global political lexicon the notion of a 'near-Arctic power'. In this way Beijing essentially internationalised a strategic theatre in which the US traditionally enjoyed primacy. The policy underscored China's commitment to enhancing its Arctic footprint and investing in the development of Arctic riches. This placed Beijing on Trump's backdoor step.

Strategic shifts during the first Trump administration—from the implosion of the INF Treaty to the China threat more broadly—served to bolster US interest in Greenland. This strategic island presented a panacea for many problems that Trump's America was facing.

Various official policies developed in the first Trump administration also explain the Greenland obsession. Trump's world view does not include consideration of climate change. Again, depending on your politics, either the world is warming because of human activity (emissions) or it is not. For some, the Earth is coming out of the most recent ice age—to take an extremely long view of things. Nonetheless, Trump views climate change as (quote) 'a hoax'. So, it is unsurprising he withdrew the US from the Paris Agreement.[20] The Paris Agreement is a legally binding commitment to reducing greenhouse emissions. Of interest is the fact that neither of the polar regions (Arctic or Antarctic) are referenced in the climate agreement. You would think they are obvious bellwethers of a warming climate. Unlocking resources under icesheets is easier (and cheaper) if there's less ice in the way. Given the Trump administration's interest in Greenland's resource wealth, one would assume an ice-free environment is rather useful. At least it helps the business case.

Another Trump administration policy was to tighten the screws on NATO. As early as 2017, Trump was asking NATO allies and partners to 'pay their fair share'. Free-riding on US military provisions or Washington's nuclear umbrella was to stop under the Trump White House. Denmark's defence footprint which Greenland hosts is often touted by the former as the nation's 'yuge' contribution to NATO. It is in fact a footprint laid down largely by US military servicemen and women, and mostly paid for by the Pentagon purse.

The unofficial yet consistently referenced policy for the first Trump administration was the Monroe Doctrine.[21] As previously noted, the Monroe Doctrine essentially states that the Americas are not open to (further) European colonisation. Trump's administration indeed possessed a willingness to invoke the Monroe Doctrine as a tool for US foreign policy, specifically in relation to the perceived influence of other nations in North America—of which Greenland is part. Trump's National Security Advisor John Bolton confirmed as much, stating that 'in this administration, we're not afraid to use the word Monroe Doctrine'.[22]

Then there was Trump's National Security Strategy (NSS). The 2019 NSS structured security across four key areas: protect the homeland, the American people, and the American way of life; promote American prosperity; preserve peace through strength; and advance American influence.[23] All four had applicable utility to Greenland. Greenland's geostrategic location serves as a buffer for threats bearing down on the US homeland from the North Atlantic. But, of course, advancing American influence was the name of the game for Trump's Greenland quest. He was not alone. Xi Jinping's China and Vladimir Putin's Russia had very real (and enduring) Arctic visions.

Another policy of the first Trump administration with clear relevance to Greenland was the Memorandum on Safeguarding US National Interests in the Arctic and Antarctic Regions.[24] This document triggered the reinvigoration of Washington's polar capabilities. At least, that was the intent, though the polar security cutter (icebreaker) programme and broader enhancement of the US at the poles wavered under the Biden administration. The memorandum ordered officials to scope new basing options for US polar assets (icebreakers, intelligence hubs, aviation and drone capabilities). No doubt, Greenland's valuable real estate played a unique role in many internal (tippy-top secret) policy planning sessions.

Alas, on 20 January 2021, Trump's term ended. As they say, 'time waits for no one' and, indeed, the world kept turning. The Biden administration substantially reframed Washington's reputation in the Arctic. Climate change was back on the agenda, the US signed onto the Paris Agreement again, and worked to ban swathes of Alaskan (and offshore Arctic) land from being tapped for oil and gas. But soon enough US Arctic interest waned, when war in Europe (Ukraine) drew the White House's attention as did 'exiting' the Middle East. During this time, the Chinese upped bilateral drills with Russia and in October 2024, for the first time in history, Chinese Coast Guard vessels entered the Arctic Ocean.

I digress: back to Trump. President Donald J. Trump returned to the White House to kick off his second presidential term on 20 January 2025. A lot appeared to rhyme with the first term, but something was rather different. A much more bullish and frank discourse flew out of the White House, via social media, into the world. Taking plenty of lessons from Ronald Reagan, Trump appeared to embody Reagan's adage 'when you can't make them see the light, make them feel the heat'. This was certainly the case with Greenland round two.

Less than a fortnight prior to his inauguration, Trump dispatched his son Donald Trump Jnr to Greenland. Trump Snr didn't have the keys to the White House yet, but the island was calling. Of course, any savvy real estate player is going to send someone to 'inspect' a property prior to purchase. Trump Jnr's visit was uncovered and explained away as a 'private' visit, with the Greenlandic and Danish governments quick to point out that no official meetings took place.

Next, it was Secretary of State Marco Rubio's turn to promote the second Trump administration's Greenland interest. Just eight days into his job, and swiftly on the back of Trump's inauguration, Rubio sat down to explain just what US foreign policy was going to look like. He began with the big-picture stuff: the Arctic is melting and shipping lanes are opening, resources are easier to access, China and Russia are partnering up, all is quite dire. Rubio noted that the 'energy that's going to be produced under President Trump' needs to use these new Arctic shipping lanes. Consequently, the US needs 'to be able to defend' the Arctic.[25]

In a masterstroke of diplomatic work, Rubio linked US policy towards the Panama Canal with its Greenland policy. The common denominator: China. Rubio argued it is 'completely realistic to believe that the Chinese will eventually—maybe even in the short term—try to do in Greenland what they have done at the Panama Canal and in other places, and that is install facilities that give them access to the Arctic with the cover of a Chinese company'. For Rubio, the president's point was simply that 'Denmark can't stop [China]; they would rely on the United States to do so.'

Providing a clear insight into Team Trump's thinking on Greenland, Rubio pointed to the US being on 'the hook' to protect Greenland already by way of the extant Defense Agreement, so it made sense to 'have more control over what happens there'. It is difficult to argue with that.

Trump's Greenland mission continued to gather speed with the SLOTUS-cum-VP-led visit to the island. While scaled down to accommodate a slimmer schedule, VP Vance's Greenland visit made further waves. In a public address at the Pituffik Space Base, staffed by US, Greenlandic and Danish nationals, the VP tore into Denmark. He argued the Danes had 'not done a good job' in Greenland and reiterated Trump's offer to Greenland to join the US. Vance told the Danes they had 'underinvested in the people of Greenland, and … underinvested in the security architecture of [an] incredible, beautiful landmass filled with incredible people'.[26]

The (US) head of the base scrambled in the days following the VP visit to smooth over the discontent seeded in the small military base team. She was fired for doing so. The Danish government also took issue with this brazen 'join us' pitch from the VP. Danish Foreign Minister Lars

Løkke Rasmussen responded that Denmark did 'not appreciate the tone' of the VP's remarks, adding, it was 'not how you speak to your close allies'.[27] Right as this may be, it appeared the Danish government had not fully grasped the intensified Reaganesque flair of the second Trump administration. The comments underscore the difficult position Denmark finds herself in—on one hand, needing to defend a strategic section of its kingdom and, on the other, needing to keep her most important defence ally on side.

In March 2025, Trump gave a monumental address to Congress. Many topics were covered, but the special message to the 'incredible people of Greenland' was certainly a highlight. Trump stated: 'We strongly support your right to determine your own future, and, if you choose, we welcome you into the United States of America. Speaking to the joint assembly, Trump framed his Greenlandic interest in terms of the US needing it for 'national security and even international security'. He continued: 'we're working with everybody involved to try and get it. But we need it, really, for international world security. And I think we're going to get it. One way or the other, we're going to get it.' Focusing back his remarks on the people of Greenland, Trump stated: 'We will keep you safe. We will make you rich. And together, we will take Greenland to heights like you have never thought possible before.'[28]

THE ART OF A (GREEN) DEAL

It was truly a sight to be seen. A sitting US president making the case in Congress for 'one way or the other' taking a slice of the Kingdom of Denmark—a long-standing ally, friend and trusted partner.

Trump did not relent. A day before Greenlanders were set to vote in their national 2025 parliamentary elections, Trump took to social media again. On 10 March, President Trump posted that the US 'strongly supports the people of Greenland's right to determine their own future. We will continue to KEEP YOU SAFE, as we have since World War II. We are ready to INVEST BILLIONS OF DOLLARS to create new jobs and MAKE YOU RICH.'[29]

The new Greenlandic government got its feet under the desk and even had a royal visit from King Frederik X (trivia point—he met his Aussie wife, Queen Mary, in an Australian pub). For all intents and purposes, the ensuing very public coverage portrayed a sense of unity and calm, with not a Trump Tower in sight.

However, within days of the king's visit, the US was back in Greenland. This was another 'private' delegation, incidentally led by the former chief of staff for the Office of International Affairs at the Department of Energy during the first Trump administration. The group included heads of major US energy firms—Critical Metals Corp, Cogency Power, American Renewable Metals and Refacture, and GreenMet. The delegation head clarified he was 'not trying to do anything crazy like orchestrate a purchase or acquisition of Greenland by the United States'.[30] Phew.

Trump continues to state there is a 'good possibility' the US will 'get' Greenland without using military force. However, he won't take the option off the table.[31] Anyone who has worked in the world of big business will recognise this mentality. The veiled threat, coupled with a vague sense of opportunity. When someone tells you who they are, believe them. Trump is a businessman turned president. Let's go back to his roots, to his word, and consider Trump's Greenland quest in terms of the business deal it appears to be.

Armed with a copy of *The Art of the Deal*, let's dig in. Right off the bat, Trump tells us, 'I like making deals, preferably big deals. That's how I get my kicks.' The world's largest island is quite the deal. The use of social media to poke and prod the Danes is likely a source of entertainment for Trump. Much of the international media community goes wild for any Trump tweet, the more outlandish the better.

Trump writes: 'you can't be imaginative or entrepreneurial if you've got too much structure. I prefer to come to work each day and just see what develops.' Don't we all? This aptly captures the sense that there might not always be a plan when it comes to Greenland. It is unclear if Trump's advisors and subject matter experts like international law savants are read into his plans before he hits 'post'. I would hazard a guess and say not. However, for a US president to embody this is chaotic for the free world, to say the least.

Is 'owning' Greenland really the end goal for Trump? It may not be. In *The Art of the Deal* he states: 'I aim very high, and then I just keep pushing and pushing and pushing to get what I'm after. Sometimes I settle for less than I sought, but in most cases I still end up with what I want.' This is an age-old negotiation tactic. Incidentally, Russian leaders are known to utilise such maximalist approaches in negotiations. Maybe Trump doesn't really want all of Greenland; just more freedoms to the north of the island? An enlarged US defence base and cheaper 'rent'?

Trump's related business advice is to 'maximise your options'. He notes: 'I never get too attached to one deal or one approach. For starters, I keep a lot of balls in the air.' There are no doubt plenty of options for the Greenland question in Trump's mind. Could he be considering playing off NATO with member Denmark? NATO is an important identifier for the Danes on the international stage, though fiscally they aren't paying a 2 per cent of GDP contribution and won't likely get anywhere near 5 per cent. Loosening their grip on Greenland might yet be an option floated.

In *The Art of the Deal*, Trump recommends using leverage. Trump writes, 'the worst thing you can possibly do in a deal is seem desperate to make it. That makes the other guy smell blood, and then you're dead. The best thing you can do is deal from strength, and leverage is the biggest strength you can have. Leverage is having something the other guy wants. Or better yet, needs. Or best of all, simply can't do without.' Now, this is *interesting*. US leverage over Denmark could be the defence Washington provides that country. Copenhagen often cites the US as Denmark's most important security partner. But Washington is really Denmark's most important security *provider*. This is some serious leverage. Trump could pull the pin on this. When it comes to Greenland, this is doubly true. US security and defence commitments are all that is standing between schools teaching Mandarin or Russian throughout Greenland. That is, of course, if China and Moscow even have such designs on the island. Leverage is quite possibly the foundational element of Trump's Greenland strategy. He has it in spades.

Why do we have such a 'unique' variant of presidential communication when it comes to designs on Greenland? Trump tells us exactly why. He writes: 'the final key to the way I promote is bravado … a little hyperbole never hurts. People want to believe that something is the biggest and the greatest and the most spectacular. I call it truthful hyperbole. It's an innocent form of exaggeration—and a very effective form of promotion.' If I were Greenlandic, I'd be requesting payment up front for any promises made or deals negotiated.

If you are brave enough, feel free to continue with *The Art of the Deal*. Wild, brash and audacious though the

Trump interest in Greenland may be, we can't say it's not deeply *logical*. Indeed, for the US to develop a deeper relationship with the North American island is just common sense. Pure and simple. Nuuk, Greenland's capital, is closer to New York than it is to Copenhagen. Even John Lennon grasped the geography of it. When asked by a reporter 'how did you find America?', he quipped: 'turn left at Greenland'.[32]

Sure, it is hard to deny geography. But it is even harder to deny the immutable right Greenlandic people possess to self-determination. With less bravado, Trump may be able to salvage this 'deal'. And he'd first have to wait on Greenland's independence movement to get on with it.

What is lost in much of Trump's Greenland discourse is the will and want of Greenland. When it is included, it is often done so incorrectly. Polls are wrongly interpreted in major global news outlets to suit the narrative that Greenland dislikes Trump and does not value the US relationship. This is far from the truth.

Donald J. Trump is not the first person to float the notion of the US 'owning' Greenland. He will not be the last. What Trump does afford Greenland is best termed the 'Trump Bump'. Greenland finds itself on the map, in the headlines, when Trump is in power. Just look at Google trends: these don't lie. Figure 8.1 captures the first Trump Bump, when global searches for 'Greenland' spiked in February 2019.

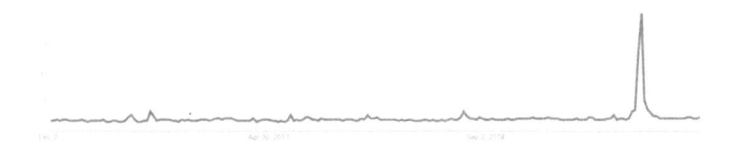

Figure 8.1: First Trump administration Trump Bump for Greenland. This illustrates Google search activity worldwide for 'Greenland'.

Lo and behold, the second Trump administration also produced a clear Trump Bump for Greenland in January 2025 (see Figure 8.2). The world's Google users appear to have jumped online to learn about 'Greenland' after hearing Trump talk about it.

Figure 8.2: Second Trump administration Trump Bump for Greenland. This illustrates Google search activity worldwide for 'Greenland'.

Beyond these two instances of heightened internet attention on Greenland, it clearly doesn't, and didn't, feature on too many people's radars. Depending on your perspective, this is either a good thing or a bad thing. Greenland can't afford to sink away into irrelevance and absence in the world, not when the Arctic arena is becoming so hotly contested and increasingly crowded. Peace through strength, as Trump says. It would appear the US is set to remain a valuable partner, if not protector, of Greenland.

Greenland's isolation was once its security blanket, but strategic competition today has all but collapsed the idea of distance and physical isolation. For instance, a cyber-attack on Greenlandic civil infrastructure, such as power or communications, would cripple the modern society that flourishes on the island.

Constant developments in Trump's America make its Greenland policy difficult to predict. There is the downright wacky—like the February 2025 Bill before Congress to enter negotiations to acquire Greenland and rename it 'Red, White, and Blueland'.[33] Then there are the perfectly reasonable Acts like those supporting Greenlandic resource exploration activities and extraction plans.

'Fake news' is increasingly rearing its ugly head in the Trump discourse on Greenland. Often trotted out is a rather misunderstood poll. The opinion poll in question is the one widely shared along the lines of '85% of Greenlanders do not wish to become part of the US'.[34] This is a misrepresentation of the data. And it does matter. The poll asked the question: Do you want Greenland to leave Denmark and become part of the United States? This is a loaded question in respect of the Greenlandic community. It is two questions in one. Greenlanders want to leave Denmark; they just aren't aligned in terms of the timeline. The framing of the question provides no option for independence, and so, of course, it is a case of 'the devil you know'.

There was much more data not shared; perhaps the less 'anti-Trump' findings wouldn't sell newspapers. Forty-five per cent of respondents viewed President Trump's interest in Greenland as a threat, and this was published widely. But 43 per cent saw Trump's interest in Greenland as an opportunity. Almost equal, but one is more ominous. And ominous garners internet clicks.

Independence is unshakeable for Greenlanders: 56 per cent would vote 'yes' to Greenlandic independence if a referendum were held today. That's without clarity over their economic future. Of interest, especially given the narrow focus of the poll's findings in the news, is the fact that a small majority 'agree or mostly agree' that Denmark should continue to support an independent Greenland financially. Not really the story Denmark is looking to get out there.

Overall, there is method to the madness when it comes to Trump's Greenland foray. US strategic interests are plainly threatened, and Washington has the opportunity (dare I say, leverage) to secure itself by strengthening Greenland. Whether this is done in partnership with Denmark, or Greenland (post-independence), or in tandem with both, remains to be seen.

All the bravado of unilateral 'grabs' and plans to 'buy' Greenland might be just that—bravado. Or Trump may push and push on the issue, drawing third parties like NATO into the spat. This would at least force stakeholders to the negotiation table, which may also be a perfectly adequate outcome for Trump.

Of course, you don't need to own or buy something to *control* it. Perhaps control is the real endgame here. Who knows. Considering future scenarios is the best part of any geopolitical challenge for political nerds, and fleshing out the trajectories of security problems is a booming business. If you are good at it, that is.

So let's look at some possible futures.

9

Four Scenarios

At 0600 President Donald J. Trump took to his 'truth social' network to declare: 'Greenland now belongs to the United States of America.' His post continued: 'Greenland is such a tremendous asset, the best minerals in the world.' Denmark's prime minister was woken by edgy staffers: 'NATO Secretary General is on the line, and, ma'am, Greenland has gone dark.'

Operation Frostbite had begun just hours earlier. Under the guise of a routine Arctic capability training mission, US Marines left the Pituffik Space Base compound. Meanwhile, US Special Forces rendezvoused at Greenland's Ministry of Justice in downtown Nuuk where most of the island's 150 police officers had gathered for a training retreat.

US forces also went from door to door to contain the 100 or so civilian and military personnel based at Denmark's Joint Arctic Command in Nuuk. By dawn, US forces had secured the airport, the port of Nuuk, and all other southern access points to the island. And, then, Greenland's internet went down.

Much of the local community gathered in Nuuk City Hall. US State Department representatives urged calm and offered a short presentation. 'Denmark has forsaken you and your children; we are here to ensure the next generation of Greenlandic people has secure work, unrestricted education opportunities, and enhanced social services,' the representatives explained.

A Greenlandic interpreter anxiously translated the message for the community huddled in the hall. 'About time,' yelled someone from the crowd. 'Resist!' screamed another, and a small group appeared to start a chant to that effect. US officials closed the meeting and implemented a curfew.

Meanwhile, Russian intelligence services had got word of Washington's mission. Moscow deployed warships and nuclear-armed submarines from nearby Kola Peninsula. Fearful of a crumbling strategic balance in its Arctic neighbourhood, Russia announced its presence was required to ensure regional stability.

Russia's 'no limits' partnership with Beijing meant intelligence was swifty shared with China. Beijing urged Washington to adhere to international law and immediately called for an emergency meeting of the United Nations Security Council (UNSC).

By 1800, Nuuk's streets were empty. The US Coast Guard arrived and announced a maritime exclusion zone around the east and west of Greenland. Greenland's airspace was also closed to non-US aircraft.

Some Greenlanders hatched plans to protest, while others saw opportunity in Washington. Denmark's parliament voted to sanction the US. Its military sat with bated breath waiting for orders, knowing full well they'd likely not come. In the days that followed, NATO called an emergency meeting. In Brussels, France and Germany condemned Washington, but Hungary, Poland and Turkey sat silent.

Meanwhile, the UNSC was unable to issue a condemnation for Washington's actions in Greenland, let alone agree to a resolution on the use of force. The US vetoed all attempts. India's president called for Denmark and the US to come together, in peace, to talk. Australia offered to broker the discussions.

Then, one week later, Nuuk awoke to chaos. Overnight, a small resistance group had cut power to the newly erected US command in Nuuk. The group also targeted the port of Nuuk, sabotaging fuel storage for US assets. Back in Washington, Congress passed the H.R. 1161 bill.

Greenland was officially Red, White and Blueland.

Quite the scenario, don't you think? Fiction writing is not my strong suit, but if it does have potential, please do let me know (or, rather, my agent). Alas, you've picked up this book for non-fiction geopolitical analysis and futures—and that is exactly what I promised to deliver. What follows is the 'real' four scenarios I have in mind for how Trump's interest in Greenland will play out.

Scenario I: A 'conscious decoupling' of Greenland and Denmark

Thanks to the international attention resulting from Trump's Greenland interest, the Greenlandic people are motivated to hasten their independence movement. Signalling their intent to break out of Denmark's orbit, and control and prosper from their own resource wealth, Greenlanders come together and decide they must first secure independence. The existing draft constitution is swiftly debated in Greenland's parliament and concluded. It is put to a referendum, along the lines of 'Do you want Greenland to be independent from the Kingdom of Denmark?' An overwhelming majority (82 per cent) vote yes. The results, and the constitution, are submitted to the Danish parliament for consideration.

The Danish parliament acknowledges the wishes of the Greenlandic people and grants independence to the island. Cognisant of economic reliance, a bilateral plan between Denmark and Greenland is agreed to, akin to the existing block grant approach, according to which the annual funding allotment is reduced as Greenland's economy strengthens thanks to external resource partnerships.

Copenhagen, initially hesitant, realises it must engage with Greenland constructively. Danish people further expect their government to act according to Greenlandic wishes. An overarching sense of shame stemming from Danish colonial rule drives this sentiment. Denmark is likely to negotiate with Greenland to maintain a semblance of Arctic presence, probably through the continued presence of the Danish Joint Arctic Command in Nuuk. Official security or defence pacts may be signed between the two states.

In any case, a lengthy transition period will likely be established in which the Danish 'grip' on the island is gradually reduced. Economic self-sufficiency will be the critical enabler of Greenland's independence journey.

During the (economic) transition period, Greenland will need to diversify its trade partners and rethink its export potential. Fishery exports aren't going to be sustainable in the long term; Greenland's critical mineral and resource wealth must be unlocked by Nuuk. A second area for economic growth and future opportunities in the social sphere is tourism. This industry is set to thrive as the nation 'opens' to the world.

Greenland's economy must not rely on just one partner. Trade agreements with the European Union and states in

Asia like Japan and South Korea, as well as China, are important for cultivating a self-sufficient, diversified economy. Here, given Greenland's geographical position, one would think its polar research offering could be bolstered. New research institutions tracking shifts in climate, currents and weather patterns could attract significant international funding. The influx of expertise could further assist the development of a new generation of Greenlandic scientists and scholars. Shipbuilding may be another industry that external partners could invest in and develop on the island.

The opening of Arctic maritime routes also presents Greenland with an opportunity to establish a strategic role in supply chains between Asia and Europe. New ports or transhipment facilities could be built. The limited manpower on the island would not be an issue per se, especially given the advances in technology today. Many ports are increasingly becoming automated, with a handful of humans simply operating large automated factories or facilities.

Denmark would fully accept Greenland's transition, from a colony to a territory, to a sovereign state. Strong cultural and trade ties would no doubt remain between the two states. Greenland would probably lean into its environmental and Inuit causes internationally, establishing itself as a global leader or bastion in protecting and promoting indigenous rights and environmental causes.

Challenges for Greenlandic independence stem more from domestic capabilities to deliver 'freedoms' equally throughout the island. While Nuuk is home to most of the Greenland population, smaller, rural and isolated settlements across the island may struggle to attract necessary fiscal support and infrastructure assistance. However, it is likely a national plan will be crafted by Greenland's parliament to deal with the 'roll-out' of independence throughout the island.

In the international community, an independent Greenland will be a special nation. While it will likely still host and rely on US forces for defence and security purposes, it will represent a progressive example of international cooperation and collaboration on issues impacting on the global community. From environmental causes to human rights, Greenland could be a 'hub' of the best parts of humanity. Don't worry, I am not about to break out in dance.

Scenario II: Independence, interrupted

Despite an overwhelming majority in favour of seeking independence, Greenland's referendum falls on deaf ears in Copenhagen. Danish interests are simply too great to accommodate the will of 57,000 people. After all, Denmark still has the leverage to call the shots. Upon receiving the formal request, the Danish government fiercely debates the issue during a special parliamentary session.

Loss of sovereignty over Greenland would substantially reduce the footprint and the remit of the Danish realm. This is an absolute no-no for the Danes. It would also remove Denmark's Arctic identity and, indeed, basis for Arctic engagement through official forums like the Arctic Council (for one thing, it no longer has territory above the Arctic Circle).

Denmark might also be facing a hefty contribution bill to NATO, and now no longer has Greenland to use as 'evidence' of a major contribution to the alliance. Greenland is a strategic territory, with historical links, of great value to Denmark. Losing it removes quite a bit of influence for Copenhagen in other forums.

To reduce the perception of (enduring) colonial ambitions, Denmark would likely state that the 2009 Act on Greenland Self-Government is more than sufficient to meet the request of Greenland for independence. The Act ensures autonomy and hands a vast number of duties to the Greenlandic government. Denmark may conjure up a peace offering of sorts to the Greenlandic people, promising to renegotiate the terms of the Act to bolster its sense of independence while remaining in the realm. Foreign and even defence affairs may be part of this compromise, handing Greenland control over an expanded list of duties.

This 'hyper-autonomy', when paired with the enduring block grant to support Greenland's economy, might provide the Greenlandic people with exactly what they desire without the nation's secession from the realm. Should Greenland push back, Copenhagen may argue that the Danish Constitution, which lists Greenland as part of the kingdom, makes it impossible for unilateral secession. Of course, the fear for Denmark may be that this movement towards independence might inspire the Faroe Islands community to follow suit. The Kingdom of Denmark would then cease to exist.

Greenland could either accept a plumped-up autonomy based on a revision of the 2009 Act, or it could come out swinging. Denmark will likely hold the line that independence is unconstitutional. Danish leverage over Greenland, namely economic, as well as support in keeping the maritime lines of communication to the island open, could be weaponised to compel Nuuk to comply.

Withholding the block grant, and defunding social services like healthcare, pensions and welfare, might be enough to foster domestic unrest on the island—forcing the Greenland government to acquiesce in a modernised autonomy arrangement. Should Greenlanders band together to reject anything less than independence, we might see protest activity. Greenland could also look to third parties for support—the US, ironically, or China, perhaps Russia—to inject themselves into the bilateral dispute. A shift towards China may already be underway, with Greenland's business and mineral resources minister (Naaja Nathanielsen) stating, on the public record, Nuuk will turn to China if others 'shun' its mining sector.[1] She noted the 'need to look elsewhere' is pressing if traditional (US or European) partners 'don't show up'. Watch this space. China and Russia no doubt would have vast interest in a foothold on the strategic island—at the Greenlandic behest.

Evicting them, however, may prove to be a challenge. But for the short-term goal of 'internationalising' the dispute, having nuclear-armed friends isn't such a bad thing. Beyond the strategic footing, China and Russia might delight in the opportunity to defend Greenland—thus signalling in real time the 'folly' of democracy and, indeed, the 'double standards' perpetrated in the liberal West.

This outcome would also make Greenland's foreign investment environment challenging, to say the least. Unease and conflict are kryptonite for investors, as this often is a precursor to permit refusals, delayed construction, and difficult export conditions for resource projects. Insurance becomes burdensome, and then there is the fear that the resource project may attract sanctions on the international market. Greenland would be a risky place to undertake business. This would, of course, undermine the nation's ability to gain self-sufficiency in economic terms. And without self-sufficiency, prosperity is stifled, and independence itself becomes shaky.

In all, even 'hyper-autonomy' for Greenland might not sit well with either community. First, it falls short of the Greenlandic people's will. Second, it is unlikely the denial of independence for Greenland aligns with modern Danish society. Denmark is quick to sell itself as a beacon of progress and fairness, and acts as often as possible as an ambassador of equality and freedom. In fact, the Danes' own official website (denmark.dk) celebrates its 'high levels' of social trust, as well as notions of community and the welfare state. Danes speak of *hygge*—chasing equality and the well-being of everybody. Denying Greenlanders independence is certainly not very *hygge*.

Scenario III: Greenland, the 51st state

There is simply no denying it: Greenland is a strategic North American island—a barren, loosely defended stepping stone into the American homeland for the enemy. Advances in military technologies have seen the development of weapons with ranges that simply collapse the distance between the US and its competitors—especially if fired over the Arctic.

A 'peace through strength' defence posture, promoted by the Trump administration, necessitates Greenland be put on war footing. This valuable piece of real estate is beautifully placed between the US and its long-standing competitor, Moscow. Any military wonk or planner would see the utility in a well-sourced forward base for US defence interests in Greenland. Should cold war shift to hot, this would also serve as a bastion front to absorb the 'hits' destined for American cities.

Even Washington's newest strategic competitor—dubbed its 'pacing threat'—China, is elbowing its way into the Arctic arena. This has come through research initiatives and partnerships—just see, for example, Yellow River Station on Svalbard (Norway), the monstrous embassy recently built in Iceland, or the immense injection of funds into Arctic universities and projects. Beijing is also physically pushing into the Arctic theatre, as per its legitimate rights under UNCLOS in the high seas of the Arctic Ocean.

But China's presence is not limited to just research vessels (which, of course, have dubious dual-use capabilities aboard), but also includes military naval and coast guard ones. Indeed, China's new coast guard laws as well as civil–military fusion laws mean that Chinese jurisdiction is no longer isolated to China's waters. Beijing is ruling the world's waves.

Just for reasons of strategic pressures at sea, it is overwhelmingly logical for the US to absorb Greenland and utilise the territory. Putting distance between rising powers like China at sea and US territorial security is likely at the heart of American defence policy today. Washington's vital national interest is to safeguard and defend American territory against external threats, to ensure the survival and prosperity of the US. Locking up Greenland sure sounds like a viable method of delivering on this goal.

Then there is the fiscal windfall beneath Greenland's ice. The reserves of critical minerals may be such that

FOUR SCENARIOS

Washington can overtake China in the production and supply of resources. Breaking Beijing's stranglehold on global supply chains in the critical mineral space is necessary to maintain strategic advantage in geopolitical terms and stay at the tippy-top of global power.

Greenland's proximity to the future of global trade routes—sea lines of communication in the Arctic linking Asia and Europe—is also a drawcard for Washington. As it won't be enough to control the goods, a global power should also have a monopoly on the avenues (routes) used to export and deliver to market.

Blood is certainly in the water when it comes to the future of the Arctic. This is the next geopolitical flashpoint of our time. In the short term the US might not move on Greenland and may fail to convince Greenlandic people to 'choose' Washington. Indeed, the Trump proposal to 'buy' Greenland may in fact become a footnote in the history books. Just as President Truman's 1946 attempt now is. But the idea of owning Greenland, as well as general global interest in the island thanks to the information age, has nonetheless planted a seed.

Perhaps in a few years' time, the US makes an offer that is acceptable to the people of Greenland. Their quest for independence is viewed increasingly as 'window dressing': the central dive is economic independence from Denmark and the enablement of a self-sufficient, enduring statehood, with fantastic living standards. Despite being unconstitutional, the autonomous Greenland government holds a referendum: 'Do you support integration with the US?'

A flurry of social media campaigns may result. Of course, the nation may simply want to integrate to access greater benefits. Greenlanders may weigh up the options, US or continued Danish ties, and come to their own conclusion that change is necessary. Or some kind of information warfare operation may in fact shape perceptions.

Denmark would likely protest against US actions. But given its lack of leverage, it may turn to the European community, the EU, to present a unified front against Washington. Sanctions might be considered; however, the EU would probably opt not to escalate the dispute. US competitors—Russia, China, Iran and the rest of the gang—would relish the US upending the 'rules-based global order'. US annexation of Greenland may also prompt heavy investment from Moscow to further bolster its Arctic frontier. The ever-feared 'Arctic arms race' would probably be a sure thing.

Many are quick to point out the NATO elephant in the room. Specifically, that Greenland, as a territory of Denmark, is covered by the Washington Treaty. So, let's dig into this. Denmark could invoke Article 4 of the Washington Treaty. This would see NATO members (probably sans the US, although there are no mechanisms to bar its attendance) meet to discuss Denmark's problem with US actions in Greenland. Sidebar: at time of writing, Danes have yet to do so.

Next could come Article 5. However, this is not necessarily going to be a military response. A reminder of NATO's Article 5 agreement: 'The Parties agree that an armed attack against one or more of them in Europe or North America shall be considered an attack against them all and consequently they agree that, if such an armed attack occurs, each of them, in exercise of the right of individual or collective self-defence recognised by Article 51 of the Charter of the United Nations, will assist the Party or Parties so attacked by taking forthwith, individually and in concert with the other Parties, such action as it deems necessary, including the use of armed force, to restore and maintain the security of the North Atlantic area. Any such armed attack and all measures taken as a result thereof shall immediately be reported to the Security Council. Such measures shall be terminated when the Security Council has taken the measures necessary to restore and maintain international peace and security.'[2]

Bit of word soup, but the high points matter. First, the US may not use force, thus raising questions about the applicability of Article 5. There have been recent debates as to what constitutes an armed attack—cyber-attacks, submarine cable destruction, and other grey-zone warfare tactics certainly broaden the scope of what is deemed an armed attack. Second, US annexation of Greenland might not necessarily result in the need to 'restore and maintain security' in the North Atlantic area. It would be difficult to argue in deliberations that the US had designs on moving through Europe after Greenland. We hope.

It could be argued that US actions in taking Greenland would strengthen the North Atlantic and thus approaches to Europe. Washington may be doing an embattled and stretched alliance a favour. Indeed, there is an implementation issue as well. Any UNSC mandate will likely be vetoed by the US.

NATO would probably be hesitant to trigger the exit of the US from the alliance. Most members host US military forces, have extremely close intelligence-sharing agreements, or possess national defence forces that rely entirely on US arms or capabilities. Furthermore, the spirit of NATO is to mount responses to threats posed to the alliance from the outside, certainly not from within. A founding member, by far the largest contributor, perhaps even the strongest component of NATO, as the aggressor? This notion does not compute.

Another avenue for support may be the EU Treaty of Lisbon. While Greenland is not a member of the EU, and while it is an Overseas Territory and Country (OCT), Denmark is a member. The relevant part of the Treaty of Lisbon reads as follows: 'if a Member State is the victim of armed aggression on its territory, the other Member States shall have towards it an obligation of aid and assistance by all the means in their power, in accordance with Article 51 of the United Nations Charter. This shall not prejudice the specific character of the security and defence policy of certain Member States. Commitments and cooperation in this area shall be consistent with commitments under the North Atlantic Treaty Organisation, which, for those States which are members of it, remains the foundation of their collective defence and the forum for its implementation.'[3]

More word soup. But this one is a little easier to digest. The Treaty of Lisbon would no doubt cover Denmark's concern over US actions in Greenland. But it would be perfectly permissible for EU member states to simply offer aid in response. Of course, any response can't 'prejudice' (damage) individual member states' security policies. Given EU member states have alliances or defence partnerships with Washington, it is unlikely many of them would agree to any decision taken under the Treaty of Lisbon against the US. Then there is the reference to NATO—if the alliance could not agree to raise an Article 5 response, then nor can the EU. The Treaty of Lisbon is quite clear on the need to be 'consistent'.

Denmark's only real play is to order Maersk to boycott the US. Maersk is one of the world's biggest shipping contractors and holds quite a large number of US Defense Department contracts. If Maersk vessels no longer entered

US ports, America's import and export sector could crumble.

Scenario IV: Status quo is Latin for 'this mess we're in' (Reagan)

If I were a betting woman I think the following is pretty on the money when it comes to Greenland's future. The status quo will endure. It will just be more present in our day-to-day life thanks to the social media era and, of course, the 'Trump Bump'. Greenland will continue its march—albeit paced—towards independence. Denmark will loosen its 'grip' following Nuuk's lead.

But this won't mean the US drops its Greenland interest. In fact, US influence might increase and yet find a happy medium for Greenland, Denmark and Washington, in respect of the island. It may all be rather boring. Cooperation, collaboration and partnership might rule the day.

In this sense, the US may bolster its footprint in defence terms at the mutual request of Greenland and Denmark, if not NATO itself. Its economic investment will probably be very welcome, especially in the critical minerals space, and potentially down the line, in the Arctic logistics and transport 'race'.

Depending on how you look at it, the US can gain in all the strategic ways it seeks to, without annexation or unilateral pressure on allies. Of course, this does not sell newspapers. Or, come to think of it, books (apologies to my publisher). US de facto control of Greenland may be enabled through vast contract agreements in areas like mining, fishing, logistics, infrastructure development, research initiatives or the tourism sector.

There are some precedents for the pathway Greenland may take as it exits the Danish orbit. The idea of Greenland entering a free association compact is a viable one. Some discussions on this point occurred in Greenland in the 1980s, and the draft constitution which the Greenland parliament is yet to debate does include a provision for the sharing of sovereignty or sovereign duties with other states.

A free association agreement typically involves a sovereign state delegating certain responsibilities, such as defence or foreign relations, to a larger partner state in exchange for security guarantees or other benefits. Arguably this is close to what Greenland currently has with Denmark. But Nuuk could formally propose this framework with Denmark, or with the US.

Existing free association agreements include those between the US and Pacific nations like Palau, the Federated States of Micronesia, and the Republic of the Marshall Islands. Or New Zealand's with the Cook Islands. A free association agreement between Greenland and Denmark would make possible the continuance of necessary economic support and access to Danish welfare systems, while achieving sovereign aims for Greenland.

Or Greenland might decide they've trialled something quite like this approach with Denmark, and it hasn't warmed their hearts. Greenland could look to form a free association with the US instead. The mutual benefit for these two partners is arguably much greater. US strategic and security interests would be bolstered through an enhanced footprint in Greenland, especially the sparsely populated northern region, and Greenland could unlock resources in a sustainable yet swift manner.

Of course, only sovereign states can enter free association agreements. So, Greenland must first achieve independence. Once independent, Greenland could explore making free association agreements with others—Canada, or New Zealand, or Russia—should they so wish. Ultimately, a free association with the US provides the most opportunity (in strategic and economic terms). The US variant of a free association agreement on offer is dubbed a Compact of Free Association.

As noted, Washington already has such compacts with the Republic of the Marshall Islands, the Federated States of Micronesia, and Palau. Their independence is fully recognised within the UN, and only various elements of defence policy and international relations are controlled by Washington. This sounds rather like Greenland's current position with Denmark. However, as it stands, the UN does not recognise Greenland as a separate sovereign state. This certainly cuts.

FOUR SCENARIOS

It is clear the Greenlandic people seek sovereignty. They plan to be recognised as an independent sovereign state by the UN. While the pathway to this, via independence from Denmark, is not easy, it is a right (confirmed by the 2009 Act) that Greenland possesses nonetheless.

Greenland could even declare unilateral independence and decline any partnership or association. First, it would need to find a way to make its economy self-sufficient, and quick. But this would take decades, if not more. Greenlandic society is heavily dependent on Danish support, and this simply can't shift overnight. Entire domestic industries (fishing, tourism, resources) need to be recalibrated and diversified.

Rapid unilateral independence would not bode too well for society, either. Most of the polls that are shared include findings along the lines of 'independence is good so long as our livelihood isn't impacted'. Livelihood would almost certainly be impacted if Denmark cut the money train. An independent Greenland, sans a military or defence capacity, would be sleeping in shifts, with one eye open. Rising China would have no qualms about 'taking' such a strategic Arctic outpost.

Slow and steady, they say, wins the race. Continuing the current pathway towards independence, while reaping the economic benefit from Denmark and working to 'open itself' up for global investment, seems to be a pretty shrewd strategy.

For what it is worth, I expect the status quo in Greenland to endure. Denmark and the US may vie to be the 'bestest' partner for Nuuk, but both will find their place in Greenland's future.

… Boring, I know.

Afterword

'Change is the only constant in life.' Well, at least according to Heraclitus. And there is no better geopolitical example today than the change under way in the Arctic—the strategic theatre, the part of the world, that Greenland exists within.

In the Arctic, a system-changing series of events is taking place. The kind of event Morgan Freeman, playing the president of the United States, describes in the criminally underrated film *Deep Impact* as an E.L.E—extinction-level event. Granted I am being slightly dramatic, but the change under way in the Arctic is going to be century-defining.

Beyond the redrawing of global trade corridors, or the carving up of resources for humanity's next millennium, the Arctic is hosting an extinction-level event in respect of the post-war global order. The current rules-based or liberal West order within which we've mostly prospered is ending. Might is right, and competitors are jostling for Arctic domination. Greenland is merely in the (very) wrong place in an especially challenging time.

If you've just flicked to the afterword for the 'cliffsnotes'—bravo. I won't disappoint you. Efforts to 'own' Greenland, whether by the Greenlandic people themselves, the Danes or Trump's America, have culminated in mixed results. Here are some lessons learnt from Greenland's storied history of conquest, colonisation, globalisation and conflict.

Lesson I: Thank your parents

Had Leif Erikson's Viking father (Erik the Red) not committed murder, he might never have discovered Greenland. And young Leif would not have ventured from Greenland to North America. Thanks to his dad, he discovered America. This matters significantly for Americans—who'd be robbed of the annual (9 October) Leif Erikson Day and related celebrations.

Lesson II: Colonialism endures

Try as Denmark might, there is a sense that Greenland is still in colonial shackles. From the annual block payment scheme to the fuzzy language in the Danish Constitution around the hoops Greenland must jump through to secede, one wonders how likely the Danes are to ever really 'let go'. They've, only in 2025, allowed Greenland to field the kingdom's Arctic Ambassador. Denmark isn't even an Arctic state without Greenland.

Lesson III: Greenland has power

Modern Greenlandic communities have been shaped by globalisation. But it is unclear whether the Inuit people have fully taken advantage of globalisation to further their own causes. Greenlanders have raised the international profile of the circumpolar Inuit community, but the globalised world could do with hearing much more about the quest for their independence. Connectivity affords Greenlanders unabated access to a global audience—they ought to use it. Where is their voice?

Lesson IV: Learn, adapt, and be ready

The Vikings might not have perished or died out had they listened and learnt from the Inuit people of Greenland. Likewise, adaptation is going to be necessary for modern Greenlandic people. They are facing down a US war machine that could certainly 'take' Greenland if it wanted to. The idea that the international community would rally a military defence of Greenland is imprudent. Just look at the liberal world's response to Russian tanks rolling into Ukraine some three years ago. It amounted to 'thoughts and prayers'. Not a single European state has put boots on the ground to defend Ukrainian territory.

Add to this problem set the sheer isolation of Greenland and its broader operational environment. It is increasingly improbable that the international community would link arms to repel a US appropriation of Greenland. Instead it might be smart policy for Nuuk to get ahead of the game and lay down its demands and non-negotiables, and share a vision of how an independent Greenlandic nation would effectively partner with the US.

⁕

So, you want to own Greenland? A millennium (and more) of humanity has tried. The island is inextricably tethered to the Inuit people. And it is not for sale. But you could invest in Greenland. You could partner with Greenland.

Trump's Greenland gambit will likely amount to intense investment and partnership. This is probably the goal, anyway: just think back to Trump's teachings in *The Art of the Deal*. Demand more than you want, negotiate a deal, and you'll probably get a perfectly acceptable outcome. The other party doesn't need to know how much you might have conceded.

Trump could easily celebrate a handsome investment partnership in critical minerals or an increased military footprint for US defence needs, once he walks back his maximalist demands to 'own' Greenland. Its mineral riches and strategic location are probably all he seeks, and preferential access to these is a much better deal given the ongoing management costs associated with 'buying' the island.

At the time of writing, in May 2025, US strategy appears unchanged. Investments are set to flow, with many US mining and resource executives racking up their frequent flyer miles to Nuuk. The US consulate in Nuuk has even started funding 'American Corner'—a curated selection of US books and periodicals, as well as films, at the University of Greenland. Soft power, baby.

Many US projects funded under the Biden administration endure too. Trade and investment cooperation, specifically in the tourism sector, is growing. Responsible development of critical minerals, funding for cross-cultural education initiatives, and collaboration in healthcare are emerging priorities.

There are also some not so collaborative developments. Various Facebook or X (formally Twitter) pages have been created since early May 2025. Titled 'Your Voice Is Important', through sponsored posts, these pages request feedback on the US's reputation in Greenland, from Pituffik Space Base to future relations.

On 6 May 2025, the *Wall Street Journal* broke news of an apparent US collection emphasis order, from Director of National Intelligence (DNI) Tulsi Gabbard.[1] Dubbed 'The Greenland Order', it asked agencies to step up intelligence activity in Greenland. Of course, this may be further evidence of the seriousness of Trump's Greenland policy. But it is also basic intelligence activity. Any diplomatic post anywhere in the world has such a mission. Allies spy on allies from allied territory every minute of every day.

Things are certainly afoot in Greenland. The US consulate in Nuuk, currently housed in Denmark's Joint Arctic Command building, is also on the move. Renovations are under way in a 3,000 square metre office space in downtown Nuuk, set to host the new US Consulate. An office the size of almost three football fields is arguably quite outsized for liaising with a nation of about 57,000 people.

Yet in the background of US visits and Trump tweets, Greenlandic independence is still on the move. It is an organic movement that predates Trump's Greenland interest. A 'Trump Bump' is evident with international interest in Greenland often peaking when his feet are beneath the resolute desk.

Something tells me this time the global interest in Greenland will outlast Trump. One hopes this is the result of Inuit self-determination to control the destiny of Greenland, and not because Greenland becomes the final nail in the coffin for our liberal-democratic rules-based order.

… The world really needs more *hygge* right now.

Notes

1. FINDING GREENLAND
   1. https://canadiangeographic.ca/articles/canada-denmark-end-50-year-whiskey-war-over-hans-island/.
   2. 'Greenland', *Britannica*, accessed 25 March 2025, https://www.britannica.com/place/Greenland.
   3. 'Greenland', *CIA World Factbook*, accessed 25 March 2025, https://www.cia.gov/the-world-factbook/countries/greenland/factsheets/#introduction.
   4. 'The chilling policy to cut Greenland's high birth rate', *The Guardian*, accessed 20 March 2025, https://www.theguardian.com/news/audio/2024/apr/19/the-chilling-policy-to-cut-greenlands-high-birth-rate-podcast.
   5. https://science.nasa.gov/resource/video-greenland-ice-mass-loss-2002-2023/.

2. THE CURIOUS CASE OF THE LOST VIKINGS
   1. https://www.smithsonianmag.com/history/why-greenland-vikings-vanished-180962119/.
   2. https://pulitzercenter.org/stories/lost-norse-why-did-greenlands-vikings-disappear.
   3. https://www.nma.gov.au/defining-moments/resources/bubonic-plague.
   4. 'Greenland's vanished Vikings', *Scientific American* 316 (6) June 2017.

5. https://www.science.org/doi/10.1126/sciadv.abm4346.
6. https://www.pnas.org/doi/10.1073/pnas.2209615120.
7. https://www.penguin.com.au/books/collapse-9780241958681.
8. https://www.houseofnames.com/au/hemingway-family-crest.
9. https://www.presidency.ucsb.edu/documents/proclamation-3610-leif-erikson-day-1964.

3. DANCES WITH DENMARK

1. For cracking reads on this historical period, see Eric Hobsbawm, *The Age of Empire* (1987); Richard Evans, *The Pursuit of Power: Europe 1815–1914* (2017); Barbara Emerson, *The First Cold War: Anglo-Russian Relations in the 19th Century* (2024); Simon Jenkins, *A Short History of Europe: From Pericles to Putin* (2019).
2. 'Greenland', Kingdom of Denmark. https://denmark.dk/people-and-culture/greenland.
3. https://education.nationalgeographic.org/resource/treaty-tordesillas/.
4. https://visitgreenland.com/articles/300-years-hans-egedes-mission-and-legacy-in-greenland/.
5. https://lutheranworld.org/news/greenland-church-and-people-rapid-transformation.
6. https://www.britannica.com/event/Treaty-of-Kiel.
7. https://www.history.com/articles/greenland-united-states-seward-cold-war.
8. US Department of State, 'Purchase of the United States Virgin Islands, 1917'.
9. Peter Thomas Ørebech, 'Terra nullius, Inuit habitation and Norse occupation, with special emphasis on the 1933 East Greenland case', *Arctic Review on Law and Politics* 7 (1) 2016. https://doi.org/10.17585/arctic.v7.262.
10. For full judgment, see https://www.worldcourts.com/pcij/eng/decisions/1933.04.05_greenland.htm.

pp. [24–40] NOTES

11. https://blogs.loc.gov/law/2019/06/greenlands-national-day-the-home-rule-act-1979-and-the-act-on-self-government-2009/.
12. References to the Home Rule Act are drawn from the English translation of the official document, found at https://www.cvce.eu/en/obj/home_rule_act_of_29_november_1978_entered_into_force_on_1_may_1979-en-541d1d6c-e3e9-4b81-b844-d95679e2e304.html.
13. The Commission's report is included in the submission referenced in note 14.
14. https://blogs.loc.gov/law/2019/06/greenlands-national-day-the-home-rule-act-1979-and-the-act-on-self-government-2009/.
15. Refences made to the Act on Greenland Self-Government of 2009 are found in the English translation of the Act as submitted to the United Nations at https://english.stm.dk/media/pgwbvkfq/notifikation-af-7-oktober-2009-til-fn-s-generalsekretaer-om-selvstyreloven.pdf.
16. https://nis.gl/wp-content/uploads/2023/07/Terms-of-reference-Historical-inquiry-into-the-relationship-between-Greenland-and-Denmark.pdf.
17. The draft constitution was published in Greenlandic and Danish only; reference to the contents is found at https://commonslibrary.parliament.uk/research-briefings/cbp-10234/.
18. https://www.veriangroup.com/news-and-insights/opinion-poll-greenland-2025.
19. https://www.world-nuclear-news.org/Articles/Denmark-and-Greenland-reach-uranium-export-agreeme.
20. U.P. Gad, 'Greenland: A post-Danish sovereign nation state in the making', *Cooperation and Conflict* 49 (1) 2014: 98–118. http://www.jstor.org/stable/45084245
21. http://research.dmi.dk/news/research-news/how-many-swimming-pools-of-water-is-greenland-losing-each-year/.

4. GREENLAND AND THE WORLD WARS

1. https://nordics.info/show/artikel/the-three-kings-meeting-in-1914.
2. Department of State, Office of the Historian, *Foreign Relations of the US: Diplomatic Papers, 1941, Europe*, vol. II, 273.
3. David Haglund, 'Greenland (1940) as an instance of Pickwickian "cooperation" between King's Ottawa and Roosevelt's Washington', *London Journal of Canadian Studies* 36 (1) 2022.
4. Department of State, Office of the Historian, *Foreign Relations of the US: Diplomatic Papers, 1941, Europe*, vol. II, 47.
5. Department of State, Office of the Historian, *Foreign Relations of the US: Diplomatic Papers, 1941, Europe*, vol. II, 49.
6. Department of State, Office of the Historian, *Foreign Relations of the US: Diplomatic Papers, 1941, Europe*, vol. II, 51.
7. Department of State, Office of the Historian, *Foreign Relations of the US: Diplomatic Papers, 1941, Europe*, vol. II, 55.
8. Department of State, Office of the Historian, *Foreign Relations of the US: Diplomatic Papers, 1941, Europe*, vol. II, 55.
9. Department of State, Office of the Historian, *Foreign Relations of the US: Diplomatic Papers, 1941, Europe*, vol. II, 59.
10 All references made to the 1941 Agreement Relating to the Defense of Greenland in this section can be found at https://www.govinfo.gov/content/pkg/STATUTE-55/pdf/STATUTE-55-Pg1245.pdf#page=1.
11. https://www.mycg.uscg.mil/News/Article/3292212/the-long-blue-line-greenlandcoast-guards-arctic-combat-zone-of-world-war-ii-194/.
12. https://www.mycg.uscg.mil/News/Article/3292212/the-long-blue-line-greenlandcoast-guards-arctic-combat-zone-of-world-war-ii-194/.
13. Clive Archer, 'The United States defence areas in Greenland', *Cooperation and Conflict* 23 (3) 1988: 123–144.

NOTES

14. Jørgen Taagholt and Jens Claus Hansen, *Greenland: Security Perspectives*. Translated by Daniel Lufkin (Fairbanks, Alaska: Arctic Research Consortium of the United States, 2001).
15. Department of State, Office of the Historian, *Foreign Relations of the US: Diplomatic Papers, 1941, Europe*, vol. II, 55.
16. Department of State, Office of the Historian, *Foreign Relations of the US: Diplomatic Papers, 1945, Europe*, vol. IV, 519.
17. For a cracking read on the Greenland Army, see David Howarth, *The Sledge Patrol: A WWII Epic of Escape, Survival, and Victory* (Portland: Lyons Press, 2018).
18. https://media.defense.gov/2023/Sep/26/2003308608/-1/-1/0/DESH_NE_GREENLAND_SLEDGE_PATROL.PDF.
19. Department of State, Office of the Historian, *Foreign Relations of the US: Diplomatic Papers, 1945, Europe*, vol. IV, 579.
20. Department of State, Office of the Historian, *Foreign Relations of the US: Diplomatic Papers, 1945, Europe*, vol. IV, 580.
21. https://history.stanford.edu/news/buying-greenland-isnt-new-idea.
22. https://www.un.org/en/about-us/history-of-the-un.
23. https://www.nato.int/cps/en/natohq/declassified_162357.htm.
24. https://collections.dartmouth.edu/arctica-beta/html/EA14-06.html.

5. PROJECT ICEWORM

1. https://www.history.com/articles/greenland-united-states-seward-cold-war.
2. All references made to the 1951 Defense of Greenland document can be found at https://avalon.law.yale.edu/20th_century/den001.asp.
3. US Department of Defense, *United States Army Research and Development: Progress Report Number Six; Camp Century*, 1964. This remastered 30-minute documentary is well worth your time, accessible via YouTube.

4. https://ahf.nuclearmuseum.org/ahf/history/camp-century/#:~:text=Although%20bureaucratic%20difficulties%20certainly%20contributed,was%20officially%20canceled%20in%201963.
5. For a deep dive into Nukey Poo, see Owen Wilkes and Robert Mann, 'The story of Nukey Poo', *Bulletin of the Atomic Scientists* 34 (8) 1978: 32–36.
6. Nikolaj Petersen, 'The Iceman that never came: Project Iceworm, the search for a NATO deterrent and Denmark, 1960–1962', *Scandinavian Journal of History* 33 (1) 2008: 75–98.
7. Petersen, 'The Iceman that never came'.
8. Petersen, 'The Iceman that never came'.
9. https://nsarchive.gwu.edu/briefing-book/nuclear-vault/2020-03-16/false-warnings-soviet-missile-attacks-during-1979-80-led-alert-actions-us-strategic-forces.
10. This section relies on official records cited in *Foreign Relations of the United States, 1964–1968*, vol. XII, *Western Europe*, 6–20.
11. Nikolaj Petersen, 'The H. C. Hansen Paper and Nuclear Weapons in Greenland', *Scandinavian Journal of History* 23 (1–2) 1998: 21–44.
12. Jørgen Taagholt and Jens Claus Hansen, *Greenland: Security Perspectives*. Translated by Daniel Lufkin (Fairbanks, Alaska: Arctic Research Consortium of the United States, 2001).
13. https://2001-2009.state.gov/documents/organization/96094.pdf.

6. CONTEMPORARY GEOPOLITICS: GREENLANDIC EDITION

1. UNCLOS is a long dull legal document, but it essentially lays down the law for our seas and assists in facilitating the establishment of rules governing the oceans and their resources. To bore yourself silly, see https://www.un.org/depts/los/convention_agreements/texts/unclos/unclos_e.pdf.

2. https://arctic-council.org.
3. https://govmin.gl/wp-content/uploads/2020/03/Greenlands_Mineral_Strategy_2020-2024.pdf.
4. https://paartoq.gl/wp-content/uploads/2024/03/Greenlands_Foreign_-Security_and_Defense_Policy_2024_2033.pdf.

7. ALL POLITICS ARE LOCAL

1. Credible insights into Greenlandic politics and the independence movement more broadly are best sourced from one of the island's two national newspapers, *Sermitsiaq*.
2. https://www.sermitsiaq.ag/samfund/selvstaendighed-kun-uden-forringelser/211956.
3. https://www.statista.com/chart/3417/4/greenlanders-who-would-want-independence/.
4. This document is only available in Greenlandic and Danish, and no official English translation was made. References made to this document and the draft Greenlandic constitution are based on an unofficial translation conducted by the author: Government of Greenland, *Report of the Commission on Self-Governance* (Nuuk: Naalakkersuisut/Government of Greenland, 2003).
5. https://www.osw.waw.pl/en/publikacje/analyses/2024-05-10/denmark-breakthrough-defence-spending.
6. https://2017-2021.state.gov/joint-statement-on-u-s-greenland-mou-and-hyperspectral-survey/.
7. https://www.highnorthnews.com/en/new-political-leader-greenland-we-are-path-towards-independence.
8. https://ec.europa.eu/commission/presscorner/detail/en/ip_23_6166.
9. Steinberg et al., *Contesting the Arctic* (London: IB Tauris, 2015).
10. https://www.usgs.gov/publications/geology-and-assessment-undiscovered-oil-and-gas-resources-east-greenland-rift-basins.

11. Alexander Hviid, *Till Kingdom Come? An Analysis of Greenland as the Danish Link to the Arctic* (Denmark: Royal Danish Defence College, 2015).
12. https://www.bbc.com/news/world-europe-60646898.
13. https://apnews.com/article/greenland-forced-contraception-lawsuit-compensation-denmark-539ef9e1e4ecd007dd34b2a024ecb0fa.
14. https://www.theguardian.com/news/audio/2024/dec/05/revisited-the-chilling-policy-to-cut-greenlands-high-birth-rate-podcast.
15. https://www.bbc.com/news/articles/ckgzl19n9eko#.
16. Hedley Bull, *The Anarchical Society: A Study of Order in World Politics* (London: Palgrave Macmillan, 1977).
17. https://researchbriefings.files.parliament.uk/documents/CBP-10234/CBP-10234.pdf.
18. https://www.reuters.com/world/europe/greenland-election-tests-independence-ambitions-us-interest-looms-2025-03-11/.
19. https://www.euractiv.com/section/politics/news/virtually-no-greenlander-wants-to-join-the-us-poll-finds/.
20. Josef Motzfeldt, 'Climate change in a Greenlandic perspective', Presentation at the 'Trans-Atlantic Climate Conference', Torshavn, Faroe Islands, 7–8 April 2008.

8. THE ART OF A (GREEN) DEAL

1. https://truthsocial.com/@realDonaldTrump/posts/113698764270730405.
2. https://2017-2021.state.gov/looking-north-sharpening-americas-arctic-focus/.
3. https://x.com/realDonaldTrump/status/1163961882945970176.
4. https://www.theguardian.com/world/2019/aug/24/donald-trump-us-consulate-greenland-denmark.
5. https://trumpwhitehouse.archives.gov/briefings-statements/remarks-president-trump-marine-one-departure-60/.

6. https://trumpwhitehouse.archives.gov/briefings-statements/remarks-president-trump-marine-one-departure-60/.
7. https://trumpwhitehouse.archives.gov/briefings-statements/remarks-president-trump-marine-one-departure-60/.
8. https://x.com/realDonaldTrump/status/1164228805562552326.
9. https://www.bbc.com/news/world-us-canada-49430537.
10. https://x.com/realDonaldTrump/status/1163603361423351808?lang=en.
11. https://www.highnorthnews.com/en/fake-ministerial-letter-greenland-adds-fuel-hybrid-attack-rumors.
12. Danish Defence Intelligence Service, *Intelligence Risk Assessment* (Copenhagen: Danish Government, 2019).
13. https://www.bbc.com/news/world-europe-52396715.
14. https://2017-2021.state.gov/secretary-michael-r-pompeo-at-a-press-availability-with-danish-foreign-minister-jeppe-kofod/.
15. https://common.usembassy.gov/wp-content/uploads/sites/91/2020/12/Common-Plan-for-U.S.-Greenland-Cooperation-1.pdf.
16. https://um.dk/-/media/other/aftaledokumenter-28-oktober-2020.ashx.
17. https://2017-2021.state.gov/briefing-with-senior-state-department-official-on-the-administrations-arctic-strategy/.
18. https://www.abc.net.au/news/2019-08-03/u.s.-pulls-out-of-soviet-era-nuclear-missile-pact-with-russia/11380242.
19. https://english.www.gov.cn/archive/white_paper/2018/01/26/content_281476026660336.htm.
20. https://unfccc.int/process-and-meetings/the-paris-agreement.
21. https://history.state.gov/milestones/1801-1829/monroe.
22. https://www.washingtonpost.com/world/2019/03/04/what-is-monroe-doctrine-john-boltons-justification-trumps-push-against-maduro/.

23. https://trumpwhitehouse.archives.gov/articles/new-national-security-strategy-new-era/.
24. https://trumpwhitehouse.archives.gov/presidential-actions/memorandum-safeguarding-u-s-national-interests-arctic-antarctic-regions/.
25. https://www.state.gov/secretary-marco-rubio-with-megyn-kelly-of-the-megyn-kelly-show/.
26. https://edition.cnn.com/2025/03/27/politics/vances-greenland-trip-trump/index.html.
27. https://www.abc.net.au/news/2025-03-30/denmark-criticises-vance-tone-in-greenland/105113854.
28. https://www.whitehouse.gov/remarks/2025/03/remarks-by-president-trump-in-joint-address-to-congress/.
29. https://x.com/trump_repost/status/1898879058840350937.
30. https://www.reuters.com/world/us-private-sector-delegation-heads-greenland-2025-04-30/.
31. https://www.nbcnews.com/news/amp/rcna198731.
32. https://www.youtube.com/watch?v=X4jW32cQn6k.
33. https://www.congress.gov/bill/119th-congress/house-bill/1161/text.
34. https://www.euractiv.com/section/politics/news/virtually-no-greenlander-wants-to-join-the-us-poll-finds/.

9. FOUR SCENARIOS

1. *Financial Times*, 'Greenland says it will turn to China if US and EU shun its mining sector', 27 May 2025.
2. https://www.nato.int/cps/en/natohq/official_texts_17120.htm.
3. https://eur-lex.europa.eu/legal-content/EN/TXT/?uri=CELEX%3A12007L%2FTXT.

AFTERWORD

1. https://www.wsj.com/world/greenland-spying-us-intelligence-809c4ef2.

Index

Act on Greenland Self-Government (2009), 3, 28–35, 94, 98, 104–6, 115, 129, 158, 171
Agreement Relating to the Defense of Greenland (1941), 45–57, 59, 60, 61
agriculture, 8, 14, 25
Alaska, 21, 81, 137
aluminium, 4, 46–7, 54, 55
American Renewable Metals and Refacture, 141
Apple, 74
arable land, 8
Arctic Council, 83–4, 125–6
Arctic Education Alliance, 132–3
Arctic region, *xiii*, 1, 32, 75–92, 103, 116, 125, 129, 130–31, 134, 174
　climate change in, 87–8, 90, 126, 134–5
　dual-use capabilities in, 78, 87, 103, 162
　hybrid war/grey-zone activities, 77, 79, 87, 130, 165
　lawfare and, 77–8, 83
　natural resources, 81, 82, 86–7, 88–9, 92, 133–4, 163
　scientific missions, 64, 78, 84, 87, 103, 162
　strategic competition in, 75, 79, 81, 85–92, 130, 134, 136, 137, 159–60, 161–3
　transit routes in, 78, 85–6, 126, 138, 156, 163
Arctic-5 states, 83
Arctic-8 states, 82, 85
army, *see* military
Art of the Deal, The (Trump and Schwartz), 121, 142–5, 176
Australia, vii, 40, 114
autonomy, 3, 19, 23, 27, 34
　Home Rule Act (1979), 3, 23–8, 39
　hyper-autonomy, 158, 160

INDEX

aviation, 32

B-52 plane crash (1968), 69–72
Ballistic Missile Early Warning System (BMEWS), 68–9
Bessel Fjord, 22
Biden, Joseph, 136, 137, 177
birth rates, 4
Black Death (1346–53), 10–11
block grant, 106, 110, 113, 116, 154–5, 159
Bluie bases, 54–5
Bolton, John, 136
border control, 31
Brun, Eske, 46, 55
Bull, Hedley, 114–15

Camp Century, 64–8
Canada, 1–2, 44, 47, 75, 81, 83, 126, 170
Cape Tobin, 55
Carlsberg Fjord, 22
cattle, 8
Central Arctic Ocean Fisheries Agreement (CAOFA), 82
charting, 32
China, 73, 75–6, 85, 117, 125, 130, 134, 136, 138–9, 144
　climate change and, 87, 103
　Coast Guard, 137, 162
　fishing, 82
　minerals and, 105, 110, 160, 163
　NEP/NSR and, 86
　rare earth elements mining, 133
　Russia, partnership with, 137, 138, 152
　scenarios and, 156, 159–60, 162–3, 171
　scientific missions, 87, 103, 162
　South Pacific and, 113–14
　Yellow River Station, 162
Christian X, King of Denmark, 48–50
Christianity, 24, 25
　Lutheranism, 2, 10, 15, 20, 21, 123
CIA World Factbook, 3
citizenship, 32, 36, 95–6, 100
climate change, 13–14, 87–8, 90, 101, 126, 134–5, 137
　natural resources and, 3, 109, 135
　scientific research, 87, 103, 156
　trade routes and, 85–6, 126, 138
coal, 3
coercive control, 111, 112
Cogency Power, 141
coil implants, 4, 111

INDEX

Cold War (1947–91), ix, 41, 60, 61–74, 76–7
   Ballistic Missile Early Warning System (BMEWS), 68–9
   GIUK gap, 91
   nuclear weapons, 59, 69–72, 133
   Project Iceworm (1959–66), 61, 66–8
Columbus, Christopher, 17
Comanche, 54
commercial diving zones, 31
Commission on the Limits of the Continental Shelf (CLCS), 82, 90
commissions
   Commission into Historical Ties (2022), 36
   Commission on Self-Government (2003), 98
   Constitutional Commission (2016–23), 36, 37, 98–104, 112, 114–15, 118, 119, 121
   Greenlandic-Danish Self-Government Commission (2004), 28–9, 30, 35–6
   Reconciliation Committee (2017), 36
   Self-Government Commission (1999–2000), 35
Common Plan for US–Greenland Cooperation (2020), 132
conservation, 25
Constitutional Commission (2016–23), 36, 37, 98–104, 112, 114–15, 118, 119, 121
contraception, 4, 111
Cook Islands, 169
Copenhagen, 129, 131
copyright, 32
Cotton, Tom, 130
courts, 24, 31, 32
Covid-19 pandemic, 10, 89
criminal justice system, 24, 31
Critical Metals Corp, 141
cross flags, 37
Cruncher Island, 55
cryolite, 4, 46–7, 54, 55
cultural affairs, 24, 25, 101
cyber-attacks, 147, 165

Danish Defence Intelligence Service, 130
Danish Institute of International Affairs, 68
Danish language, 32, 100
Danish Meteorological Institute, 40
Danish West Indies (1672–1917), 22
death penalty, 100

INDEX

Deep Impact (1998 film), 173
defence policy, 4, 25, 32, 94, 96, 104, 105, 115
   Agreement Relating to the Defense of Greenland (1941), 45–57, 59, 60, 61
   Defense of Greenland Agreement (1951), 62–4, 68, 69, 70, 71–2, 77
   Greenland in the World (2024), 89–92
   Igaliku Amendments (2004), 72–3
   NATO and, 58, 59, 62, 67, 73, 91, 104, 129, 131, 135, 143
Defense of Greenland Agreement (1951), 62–4, 68, 69, 70, 71–2, 77
demographics, 4, 35
Denmark, viii, ix, 1–3, 4, 19–40, 92, 93–121, 157–61
   Act on Greenland Self-Government (2009), 3, 28–35, 94, 98, 104–6, 115, 129, 158
   Agreement Relating to the Defense of Greenland (1941), 46, 47–53, 56–7, 59, 60
   Arctic region and, 81, 83, 89, 130–31, 174
   Constitution, 29, 35, 36, 98, 159, 174
   Constitutional Commission and, 103–4, 119
   Defense of Greenland Agreement (1951), 62–4, 68, 69, 70, 71–2, 77
   economic support of Greenland, 32, 37–8, 93, 106, 110, 113, 115–16, 154–5, 159
   Egan plan (1910), 21–2
   Greenland colony (c. 1728–1953), ix, 2–3, 4, 21–3, 99, 119, 174
   Home Rule Act (1979), 3, 23–8, 30, 31, 39
   Igaliku Amendments (2004), 72–3
   NATO spending, 104, 129, 135, 143, 158
   Nazi occupation (1940–45), 23, 42, 43, 48, 51, 56–7, 119
   reparations and, 110–11
   Seward proposal (1867), 21
   Treaty of Kiel (1814), 21, 22
   Trump, relations with, 126–9, 133, 139–41
   United States embassy, 21, 42, 44, 45, 47–50, 53, 55–7, 60, 131

INDEX

West Indies (1672–1917), 22
Whiskey War (1973–2022), 1–2
World War I (1914–18), 41–2
World War II (1939–45), 42, 44, 47
domestic violence, 94, 111
draft constitution (2023), 36, 98, 100–104, 112, 114–15, 118, 121
dual use capabilities, 78, 87, 103, 162

economy, 25, 32, 35, 37–8, 93–4, 105, 155–6
    Danish support, 32, 37–8, 93, 106, 110, 115, 113, 115–16, 154–5, 159
    self-sufficiency, 35, 92, 100, 106, 115, 117, 155–6, 160, 171
education, 24, 25, 37, 101, 106, 110, 113, 132–3, 177
Egan, Maurice, 21
Egede, Hans, 2, 10, 15, 20, 21, 123
Egedesminde, 55
electricity, 59

Ella Ø island, 55
Ellesmere Island, 1
English language, 132

environmental protection, 25, 32, 36, 78, 83, 90, 121, 156
Erik the Red, 2, 7–8, 16, 17, 174
Erik the Red's Land (1931–3), 22–3
Erikson, Leif, 17, 174
Eskimonæs, 55
European Economic Community (EEC), 39
European Union (EU), 108, 155–6, 164, 166–7
exchange rates, 32
exclusive economic zones (EEZs), 92
'Experiment, The' (1951), 110–11

family law, 31
Faroe Islands, 21, 27, 159
Federated States of Micronesia, 169, 170
finance committee, 101
financial regulation, 32
Finland, 37, 84, 125
fisheries, 4, 25, 26, 81, 82, 88, 101, 155, 169
flag, 37, 73
Folketing, 33
Force X plan (1940), 47
foreign policy, 25–6, 32, 89–92, 94, 96, 101, 105, 115, 116, 129
foreign policy committee, 101

INDEX

Foreign Relations Committee, US, 127
Forsvarets Efterretningstjeneste (FE), 130
France, 20–21
Frederick IV, King of Demark–Norway, 20
Frederik X, King of Denmark, 141
Frederiksen, Mette, 127–9
free association, 36–7, 98, 99, 101–2, 169, 170

Gabbard, Tulsi, 177
gas, 3, 81, 87, 108
general election (2025), 117, 124
Germany, 21, 22, 23
    Nazi Germany (1933–45), 23, 42, 43, 47, 48, 51, 55–7, 60, 119
globalisation, 12, 85, 174–5
goats, 8
Good Traitor, The (2020 film), 45
Greenland Army, 43, 56
Greenland
    autonomous province status (1953), 2, 23, 58, 99, 119
    Constitutional Commission (2016–23), 36, 37, 98–104, 112, 114–15, 118, 119, 121
    Danish colony (c. 1728–1953), ix, 2–3, 4, 21–3, 99, 119, 174
    defence policy, *see* defence policy
    demographics, 4, 35
    draft constitution (2023), 36, 98, 100–104, 112, 114–15, 118, 121
    EEC withdrawal (1985), 39
    flag, 37, 73
    Home Rule Act (1979), 3, 23–8, 30, 31, 39
    Home Rule referendum (1979), 24
    icesheet melt, 5, 40, 87–8, 135
    Igaliku Amendments (2004), 72–3
    independence movement, *see* independence movement
    language in, 27, 32, 36, 37, 100, 132
    Lutheranism in, 2, 10, 15, 20, 21, 123
    military forces, 43, 56
    natural resources, *see* natural resources
    Norwegian colony (1931–3), 22–3
    parliamentary democracy, 3, 24, 37

INDEX

Project Iceworm (1959–66), 61, 66–8
reparations movement in, 110–11
Self-Government Act (2009), 3, 28–35, 94, 98, 104–6, 115, 129, 158, 171
Self-Government referendum (2008), 3, 28–30, 94
United States acquisition, *see* United States acquisition of Greenland
Vikings in, ix, 2, 7–18, 20, 21
Weather War (1942–4), 42–3
World War I (1914–18), 41–2
Greenland in the World (2024) 89–92
Greenland Mineral Strategy (2020), 88
Greenland–Iceland–United Kingdom (GIUK), 91
Greenlandic language, 27, 32, 36, 37, 100
Greenlandic–Danish Self-Government Commission (2004), 28–9, 30, 35–6
GreenMet, 141
grey-zone activities, 77, 79, 87, 165

Grimsey Island, 84
Grønnedal naval base, 4, 47, 55, 63

Hans Island, 1–2
Hansen, Hans Christian, 70
healthcare, 25, 37, 101, 106, 113, 159, 177
Hemingway, Ernest, 16
Heraclitus, 173
Hitler, Adolf, 55
Home Rule Act (1979), 3, 23–8, 30, 31, 39
Home Rule referendum (1979), 24
hospitality, 25
Hotel Hans Egede, Nuuk, 123–5
Hull, Cordell, 48
hunting, 5, 25, 88, 100
hybrid war, 77, 79, 87, 130
hydrocarbons, 3, 26, 31, 81, 87, 88, 108, 137
hygge, 161, 178
hyper-autonomy, 158, 160

Iceland, 7, 8, 21, 37, 84, 119–20, 162
icesheets, 3, 5, 8, 41, 109
melting of, 5, 40, 87–8, 135, 138
Igaliku Amendments (2004), 72–3
Ikateq, 54

Inatsisartut, 3, 33, 37, 39, 94, 101, 102, 117
  Constitutional Commission (2016–23), 36, 37, 98–104, 112, 114–15, 118, 119, 121
independence movement, viii, ix, x, 3, 28, 33, 37, 89, 93–121, 154–61, 168, 171
  Constitutional Commission (2016–23), 36, 37, 98–104, 112, 114–15, 118, 119, 121
  Greenland in the World (2024) 89–92
  polling on, 37, 95, 119, 120, 145, 147–8
  Self-Government Act (2009), 3, 28–35, 94, 98, 104–6, 115, 129, 158, 171
India, 87
indigenous peoples, 39, 58, 79, 81, 83, 156
industrial injury compensation, 31
intellectual property, 32
Intercontinental Ballistic Missiles (ICBMs), 68
Intermediate Nuclear Forces Treaty (1987), 133
international relations, 101
intrauterine contraceptive devices, 4, 111
Inuit, 2, 11, 14, 17, 20, 50, 88, 108, 110–11, 174–5, 178
  reparations movement, 110–11
  Vikings, relations with, 11, 14, 17, 175
iPhone, 74
Iran, 32, 130, 164
Isua, 110
Ivigtut, 46–7, 54
ivory trade, 9, 11–12, 14–15, 120–21

Japan, 156
Jensen, Erik, 107–8
Jobs, Steve, 74
Johnson, Lyndon, 17
Joint Arctic Command, 178
judiciary, 24, 31, 32, 36

Kauffmann, Henrik, 42, 44, 45, 47–50, 53, 55–7, 60
Kennedy, John Fitzgerald, 67
King, William Lyon Mackenzie, 47
Kipisako, 55
Kvanefjeld, 110

labour market, 25
Landsstyre, 24
Landsting, 24
language, 27, 32, 36, 37, 100, 132
law committee, 101

INDEX

lawfare, 64, 77–8, 83, 105
lead, 3
Lennon, John, 145
leverage, 143–4
Library of Congress, 24
Little Danes Experiment (1951), 110–11
livestock, 8, 14
Lutheranism, 2, 10, 15, 20, 21, 123

Maersk, 167–8
marine environments, 32
maritime emergency services, 31
Marshall Islands, 169, 170
Mary, Queen consort of Denmark, 141
Medium-Range Ballistic Missiles (MRBMs), 67
Memorandum on Safeguarding (2020), 136–7
Mercator, Gerardus, 5
meteorology, 32, 42–3, 55, 103
Micronesia, 169, 170
military affairs, *see* defence policy
military forces, 43, 56
minerals, 3–4, 5, 26, 31, 38, 88, 100, 105, 106–8, 110, 155
   China and, 87, 103, 162
   European Union and, 108, 155–6
   United States and, 107–8, 132, 133, 168, 169, 177
monarchy, 36
monetary policy, 32, 94
Monroe, James, 44, 50, 57, 135–6

Napoleon I, Emperor of the French, 19, 20
Napoleonic Wars (1803–15), 20–21
Narsarsuaq, 54, 64
Nathanielsen, Naaja, 159
National Aeronautics and Space Administration (NASA), 5, 67
National Security Strategy (2019), 136
nationality, 32, 36, 95–6, 100
natural gas, 3, 81, 87, 108
natural resources, 26–7, 31, 38, 81, 82, 86–7, 92, 105–10, 121, 133–4, 155
   fisheries, 4, 25, 26, 81, 82, 88, 101, 155, 169
   hydrocarbons, 3, 26, 31, 81, 87, 88, 108, 137
   icesheet melt and, 3, 109, 135
   minerals, *see* minerals
Nazi Germany (1933–45), 23,

42, 43, 47, 48, 51, 55–7, 60, 119
neutrality, 41, 42, 47, 59, 62
New Zealand, 169, 170
North Atlantic Treaty Organization (NATO), 58, 59, 62, 67, 73, 91, 131, 149, 164–7, 168
  Danish spending, 104, 129, 135, 143, 158
North-East Greenland Sledge Patrol, 56
Northeast Passage (NEP), 85
Northern Sea Route (NSR), 85
Northwest Passage (NWP), 86, 126
Norway, 7, 9, 11, 21, 22, 37, 41, 162
  Erik the Red's Land (1931–3), 22–3
nuclear power, 61, 65, 66–8
nuclear weapons, 59, 69–72, 133–4
Nuuk, ix, 123, 128, 131, 132, 145, 157
  United States consulate, 128, 129, 132, 177, 178

oil, 3, 81, 87, 108
Oil and Mineral Strategy (2014–18), 88

Palau, 169, 170
Panama Canal, 138
Paris Agreement (2015), 135, 137
parliament, *see* Inatsisartut
parliamentary democracy, 3, 24, 37
passports, 31, 36
Peace Corps, 132
pensions, 38, 159
Permanent Court of International Justice (PCIJ), 23
Philippines, 22, 50
Pituffik Space Base, ix, 54, 64, 104, 124, 125, 132, 139, 151
platinum, 3
policing, 31
polling, 37, 95, 119, 120, 145, 147–8
Pompeo, Mike, 125–6, 129, 131–2
population, 4, 35
Portugal, 20
postal services, 52
Prins Christianssund, 55
prisons, 24, 31
Project Iceworm (1959–66), 61, 66–8
property law, 31
Putin, Vladimir, vii, 136

radioactive materials, 38
rare earth elements, 133

INDEX

Rasmussen, Lars Løkke, 139–40
Reagan, Ronald, 137, 140
Reconciliation Committee (2017), 36
Red, White, and Blueland Act (US, 2025), 147, 153
referenda, 37, 101, 154
   1979 Home Rule referendum, 24
   2008 Self-Government referendum, 3, 28–30, 94
religion, 24, 25
   Lutheranism, 2, 10, 15, 20, 21, 123
republicanism, 36
resources, *see* natural resources
roads, 31
Roanoke Colony (1585–90), 11
Roosevelt, Franklin, 47, 48–50
Rubio, Marco, 138–9
rules-based global order, 164, 178
Russian Empire (1721–1917), 21
Russian Federation (1991–), 73, 76, 81, 83, 104, 130, 134, 136, 144
   Arctic transit routes and, 78, 86
   China, partnership with, 137, 138, 152
   maximalist approach, 143
   scenarios and, 152, 159, 160, 161, 164, 170
   Ukraine War (2022–), 77, 89, 137, 175

Sands, Carla, 131
Schleswig-Holstein, 21
scientific missions, 64, 78, 84, 87, 103, 156, 162
seal pelts, 9, 15, 120–21
Self-Government Act (2009), 3, 28–35, 94, 98, 104–6, 115, 129, 158, 171
Self-Government Commission (1999–2000), 35
self-government referendum (2008), 3, 28–30, 94
self-sufficiency, 35, 92, 100, 106, 115, 117, 155–6, 160, 171
Seward, William, 21
sheep, 8
ship registration, 32
shipbuilding, 156
Sirius Patrol, 43
Siumut, 107
slave labour, 101
Smithsonian Institution, 9
social media, 126–7, 129–30, 141, 142, 168

social services, 93, 106
  education, 24, 25, 37, 101, 106, 110, 113
  healthcare, 25, 37, 101, 106, 113, 159
social welfare, 25, 159, 161, 170
Solomon Islands, 113–14
Søndre Strømfjord, 54
Sondrestrom, 64
South Korea, 156
South Pacific, 113–14, 169, 170
sovereignty, 33, 36, 44, 51, 52, 93, 96–7, 114–15, 171
Soviet Union (1922–91), 60, 67, 68, 72, 76–7, 133
Spain, 20
Status of Forces Agreement, 73
Stockholm syndrome, 111
strategic competition, 41, 73, 75, 79, 81, 85
Strategic Partnership on Sustainable Raw Materials (2023), 108
subsidies, 32, 115
succession law, 31
Suez Canal, 86
Supreme Court, 32
Svalbard, 162
Svane, Aksel, 46, 55
Sweden, 21, 37, 41, 84

tantalite, 3

Teague Field, 55
Three Kings Meeting (1914), 41–2
Thule, 55, 64, 65
Thule Air Base, 54, 64, 68–72, 73, 132
Thule culture, 20
tourism, 25, 155, 169, 177
trade, 25, 85, 105, 138
transportation, 25, 31, 101
Treaty of Kiel (1814), 21, 22
Treaty of Lisbon (2007), 166–7
Treaty of Tordesillas (1494), 20
Truman, Harry, 128, 163
Trump, Donald, vii–x, 93, 107, 119, 120, 121, 123–49, 176–8
  Art of the Deal, The (1987), 121, 142–5, 176
  climate change, views on, 126, 134–5
  Common Plan for US–Greenland Cooperation (2020), 132
  Copenhagen crisis (2019), 126–9
  Memorandum on Safeguarding (2020), 136–7
  Monroe Doctrine and, 135–6

National Security Strategy
(2019), 136
NATO, views on, 129, 135
Trump, Donald Jnr, 138
'Trump Bump', 145–6, 168, 178

U-boats, 55
Ukraine, 77, 89, 137, 175
unemployment, 110
United Kingdom, 39, 40, 44
United Nations (UN), 2, 58, 99, 170–71
   Charter (1945), 165, 167
   Commission on the Limits of the Continental Shelf (CLCS), 82, 90
   Convention on the Law of the Sea (UNCLOS), 78, 82, 162
   Paris Agreement (2015), 135, 137
   Resolution 1541 (1960), 101
   Sustainable Development Goals, 81
United States
   acquisition of Greenland, *see* United States acquisition of Greenland
   Agreement Relating to the Defense of Greenland (1941), 45–57, 59, 60, 61
   Arctic Education Alliance, 132–3
   Arctic Ocean and, 76, 77, 78, 80–81, 83
   B-52 plane crash (1968), 69–72
   buffer zone, Greenland as, 80–81, 136
   climate change policies, 134–5, 137
   Common Plan for US–Greenland Cooperation (2020), 132
   Defense of Greenland Agreement (1951), 62–4, 68, 69, 70, 71–2, 77
   Denmark embassy, 21, 42, 44, 45, 47–50, 53, 55–7, 60, 131
   Greenland consulate, 128, 129, 132, 177, 178
   hydrocarbons and, 109–10, 137
   Igaliku Amendments (2004), 72–3
   Johnson administration (1865–9), 21
   Kennedy administration (1961–3), 67
   Memorandum on Safeguarding (2020), 136–7
   military bases, *see* military bases

minerals and, 107–8, 109–10, 132, 133, 168, 169
Monroe administration (1817–25), 44, 50, 57, 135–6
National Security Strategy (2019), 136
nuclear weapons, 59, 69–72
Project Iceworm (1959–66), 61, 66–8
Red, White, and Blueland Act (2025), 147, 153
Roosevelt administration (1933–45), 45–7
South Pacific, relations with, 113–14, 169, 170
Taft administration (1909–13), 21
Truman administration (1945–53), 57–8, 62–4, 128
Trump administration, first (2017–21), 107, 125–37
Trump administration, second (2025–), vii–x, 93, 119, 120, 123–5, 137–49
World War II (1939–45), 44–6
United States acquisition of Greenland, vii–x, 21–2, 57–8, 103–4, 113, 120, 123–49, 161–8, 175–8
Egan's plan, (1910) 21–2
Seward's purchase proposal (1867), 21
Truman's purchase proposal (1946), 57–8, 163
Trump's purchase proposals (2019–20), 126–31, 146–7
Trump's purchase proposals (2024–5), 123–5, 139–49, 176
United States Coast Guard, 43, 54
United States Geological Survey (USGS), 109–10
United States military bases, ix, 54, 55, 57, 59, 61–73, 107
Bluie East 54–5
Bluie West, 54–5
Camp Century, 64–8
Grønnedal naval base, 4, 47, 55, 63
Pituffik Space Base, ix, 54, 64, 104, 124, 125, 132, 139
Thule Air Base, 54, 64, 68–72, 73, 132
United States Virgin Islands (1917–), 22
uranium, 3, 38

INDEX

Vance, James David, 124–5, 139
Vance, Usha, 123–4, 139
Vikings, ix, 2, 5, 7–18, 20, 21, 174, 175
   climate change and, 13–14, 88
   Inuit, relations with, 11, 14, 17, 175
   ivory trade, 9, 11–12, 14–15

walrus ivory, 9, 11–12, 14–15
Waltz, Mike, 124
weather balloons, 103
Weather War (1942–4), 42–3
welfare, 25, 159, 161, 170
Whiskey War (1973–2022), 1–2
wildfires, 87
witch burnings, 9
World War I (1914–18), 41–2
World War II (1939–45), 42–57
Wright, Chris, 124

Xi Jinping, 136

Yellow River Station, Svalbard, 162

zinc, 3

Northwest Passage

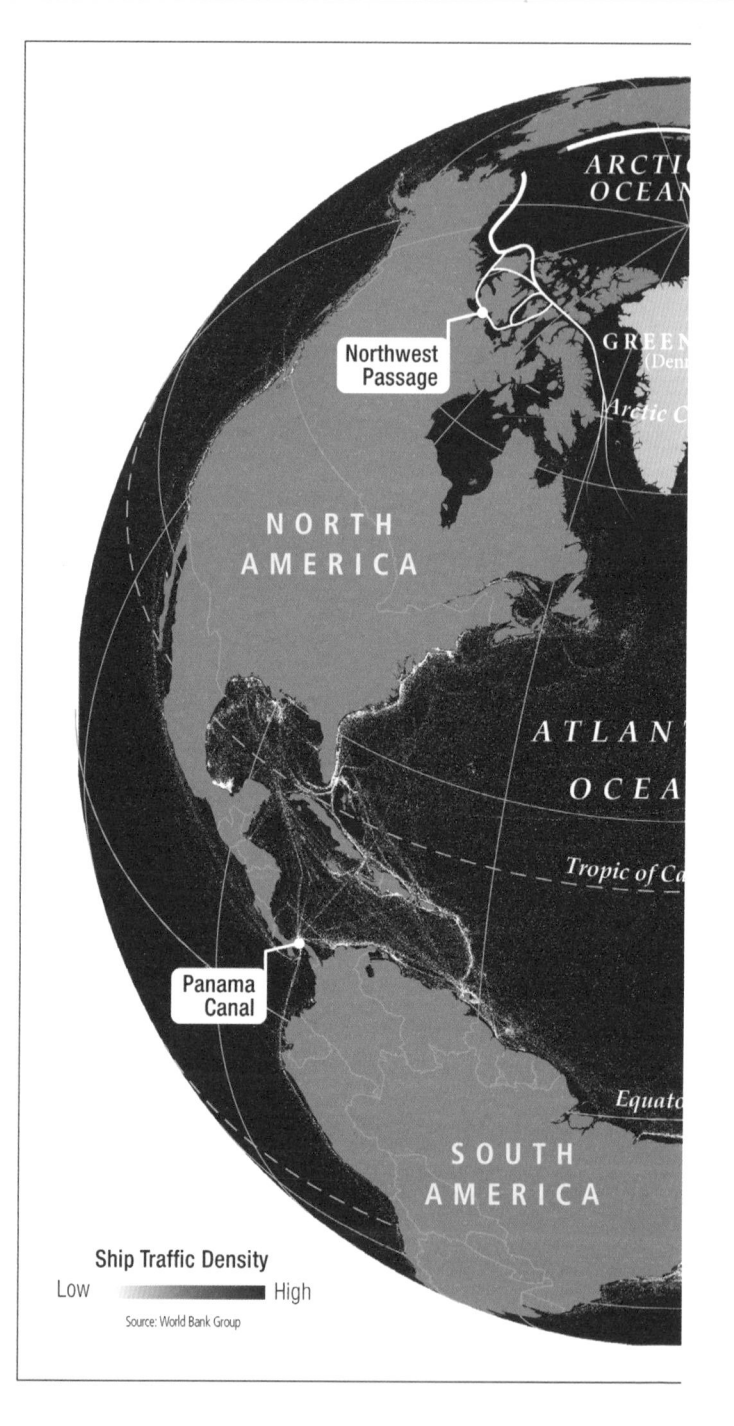

Panama Canal

ARCTIC OCEAN

GREEN(Den

Arctic C

NORTH AMERICA

ATLAN
OCEA

Tropic of Ca

Equato

SOUTH AMERICA

Ship Traffic Density
Low ▬▬▬▬ High
Source: World Bank Group